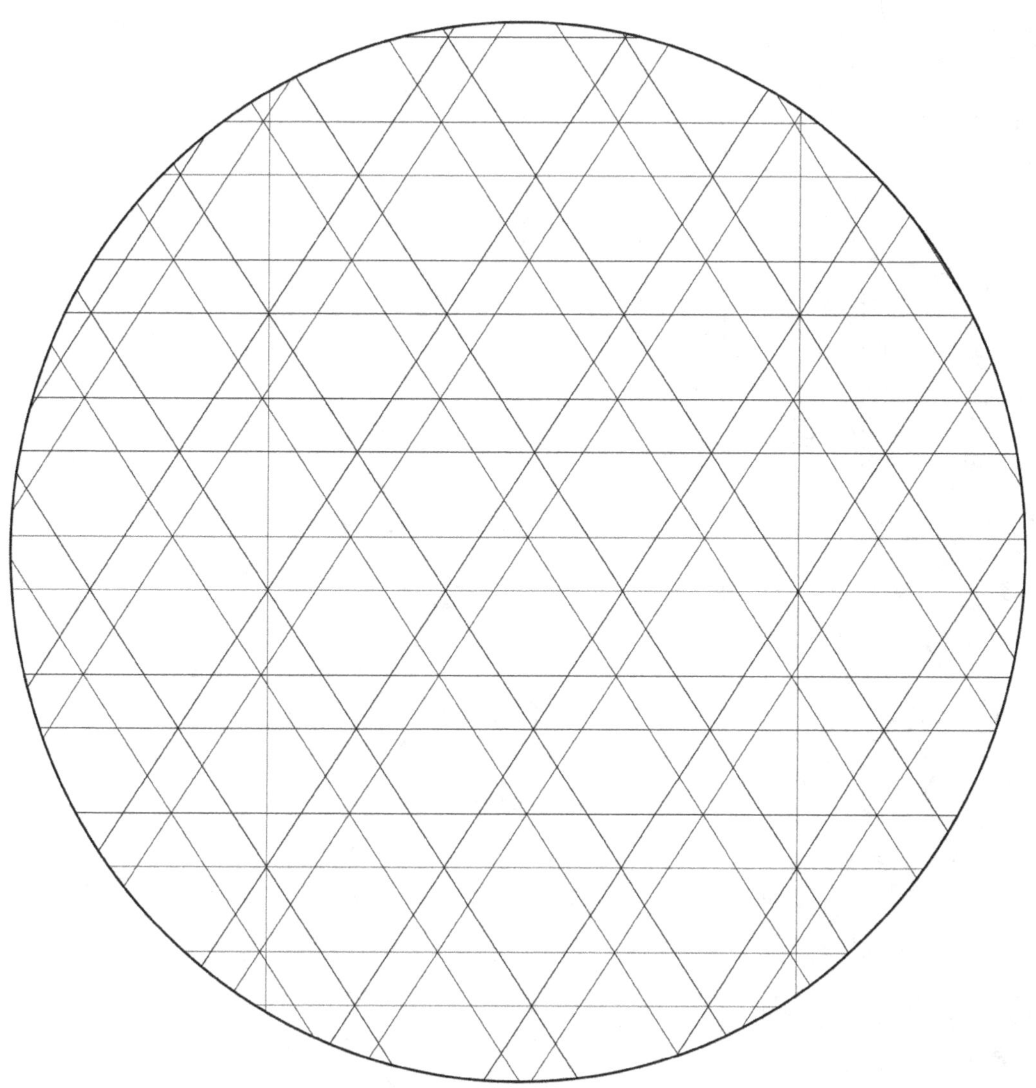

Geometric Coloring Book

Stress Relieving Designs Vol 1

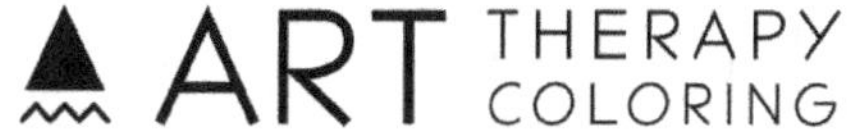

Preview of Coloring Pages

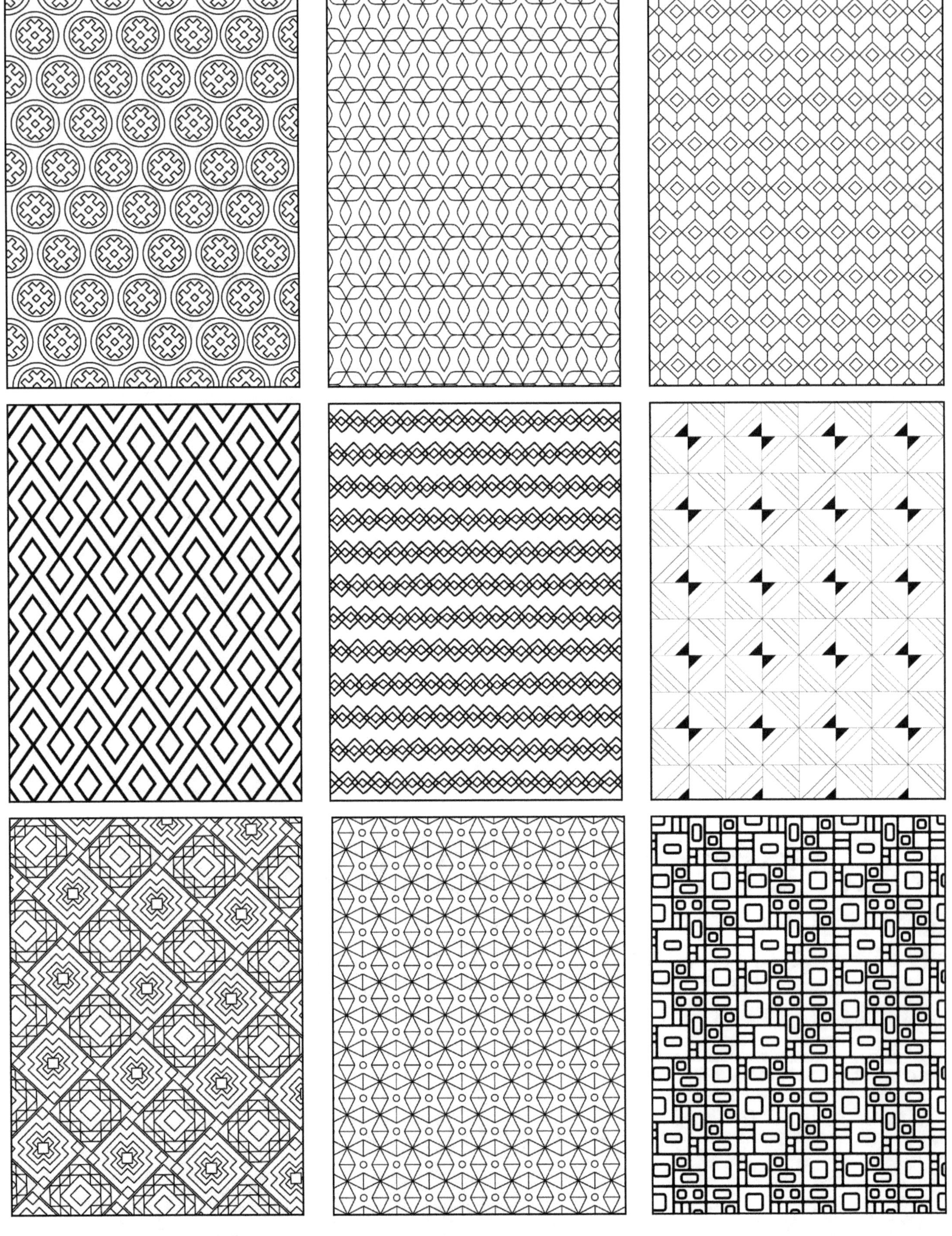

www.arttherapycoloring.com

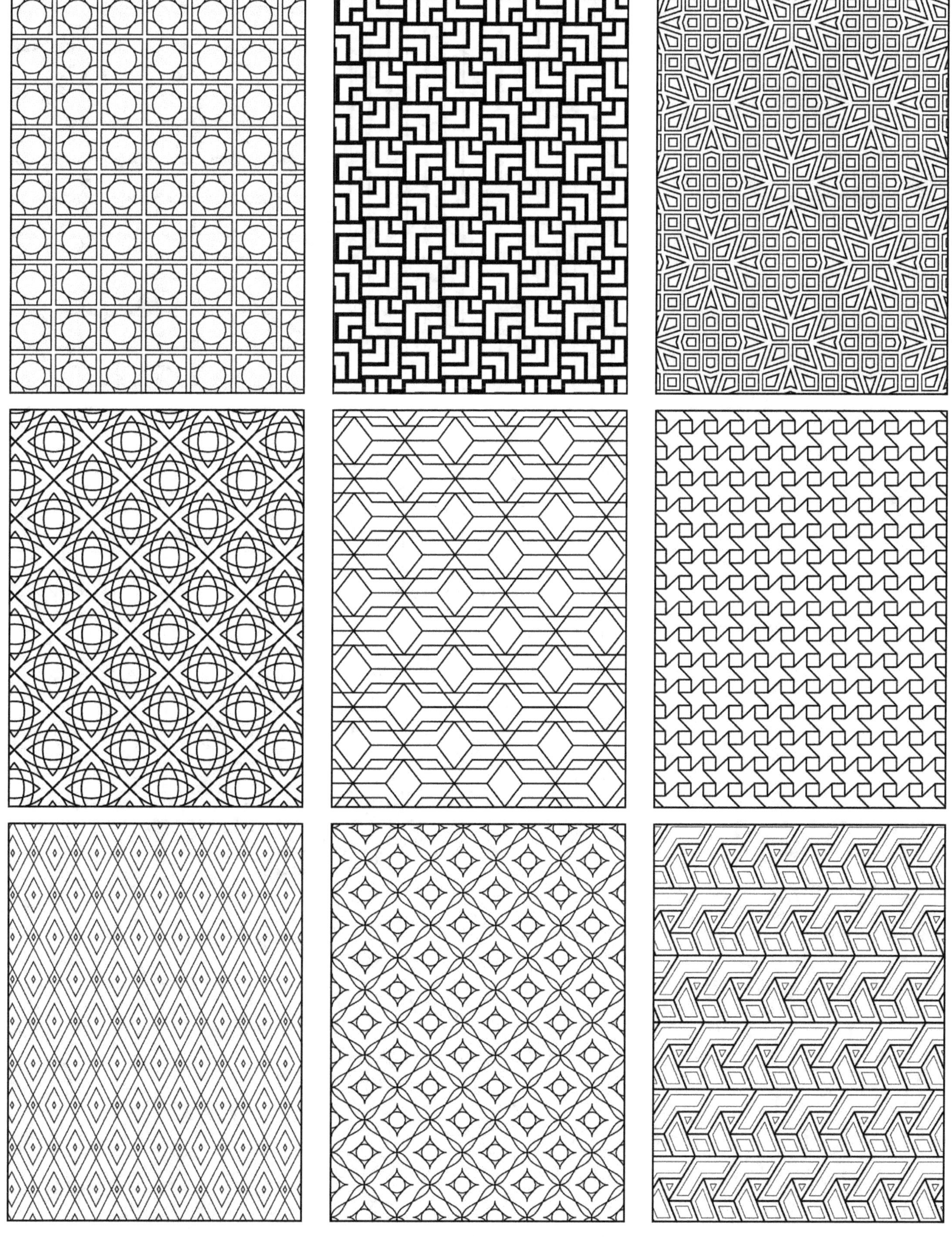

Preview of Coloring Pages

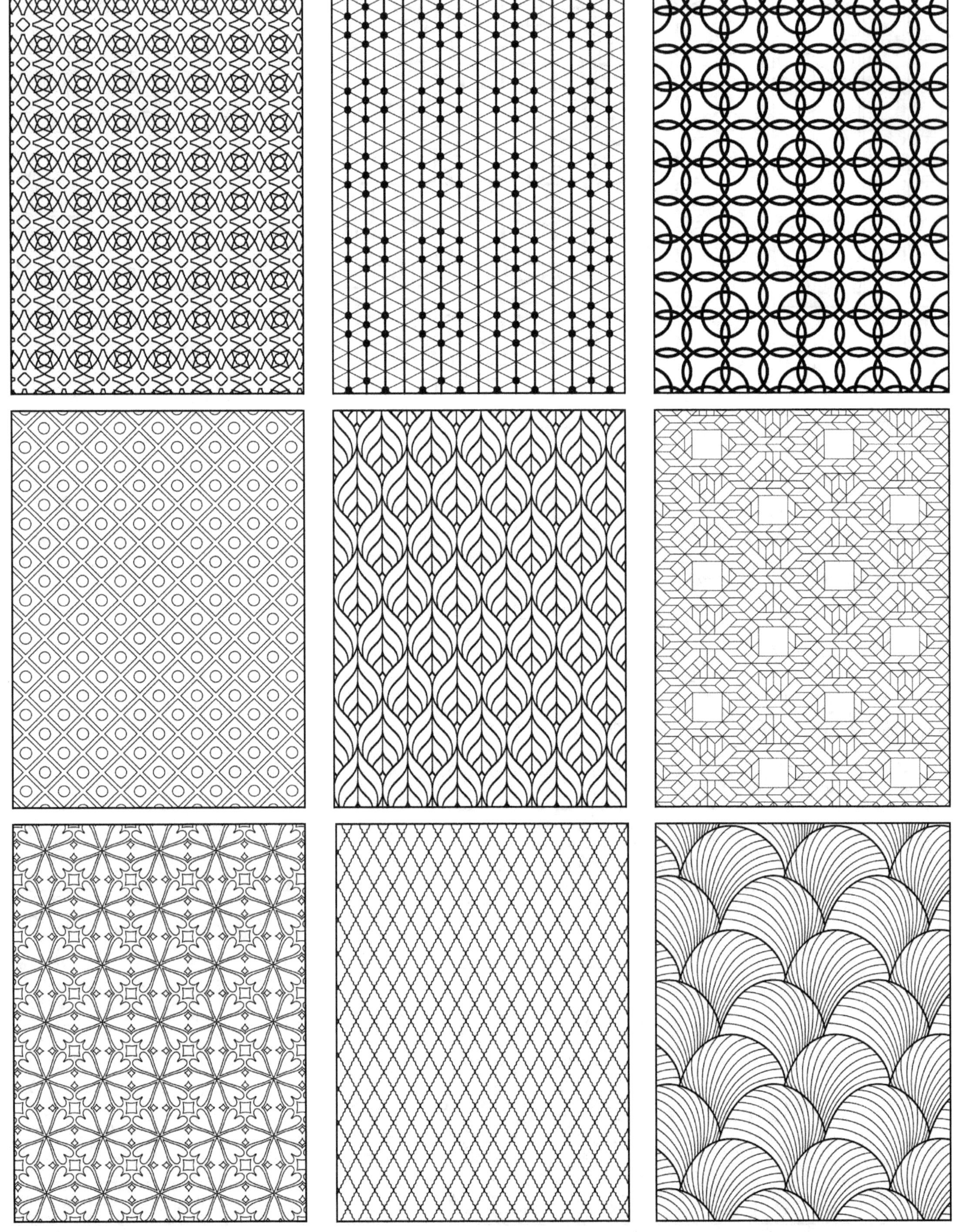

www.arttherapycoloring.com

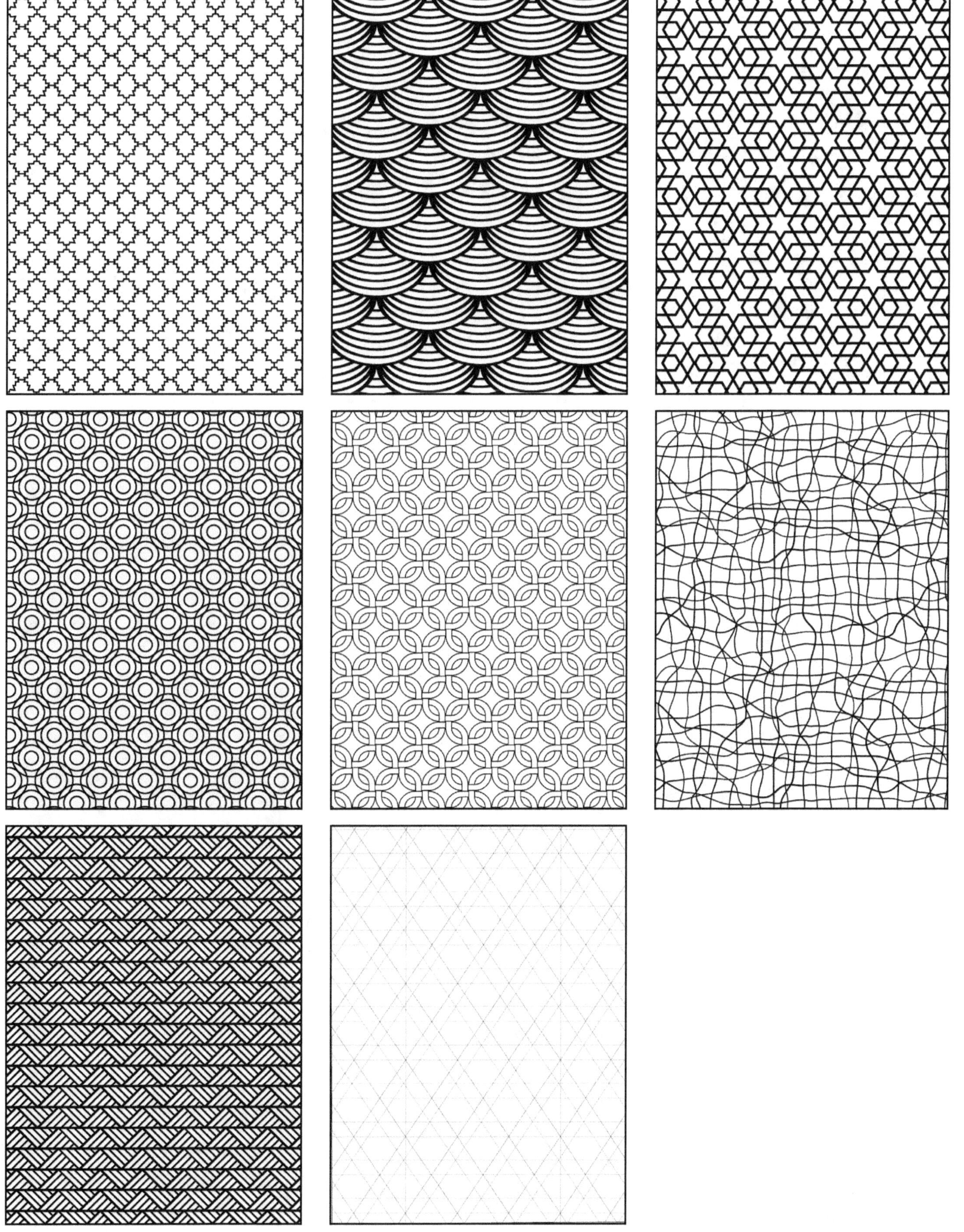

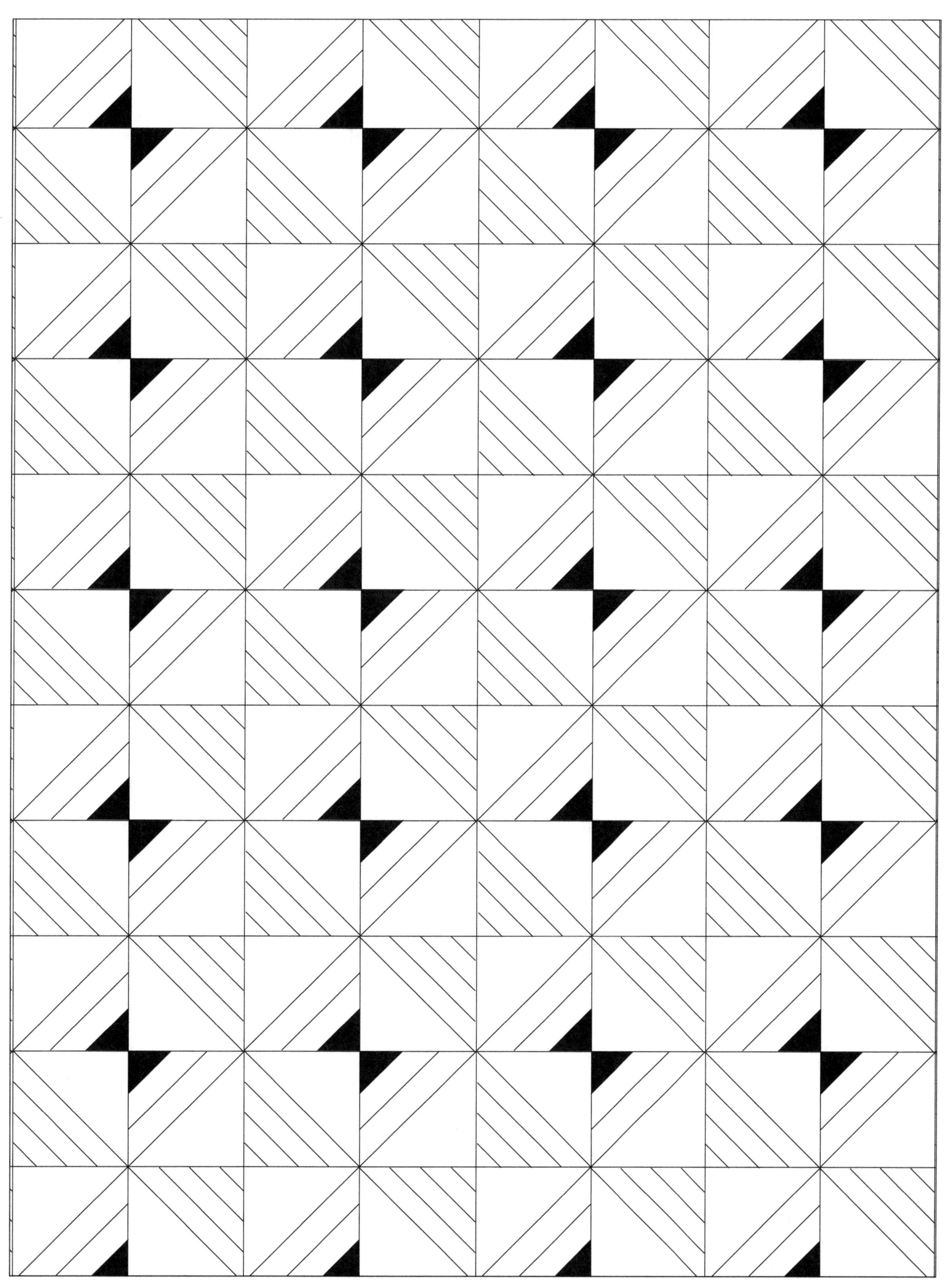

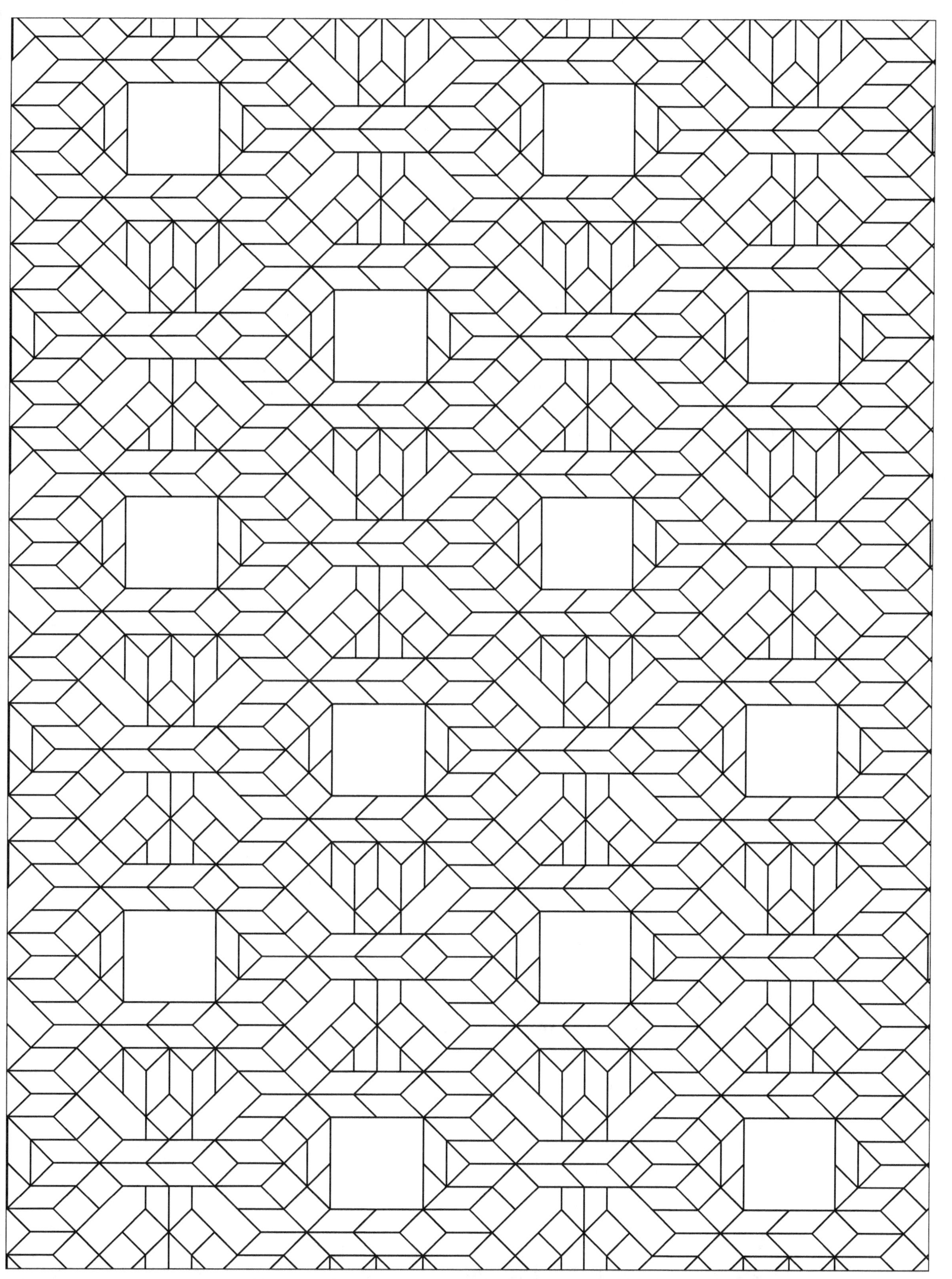

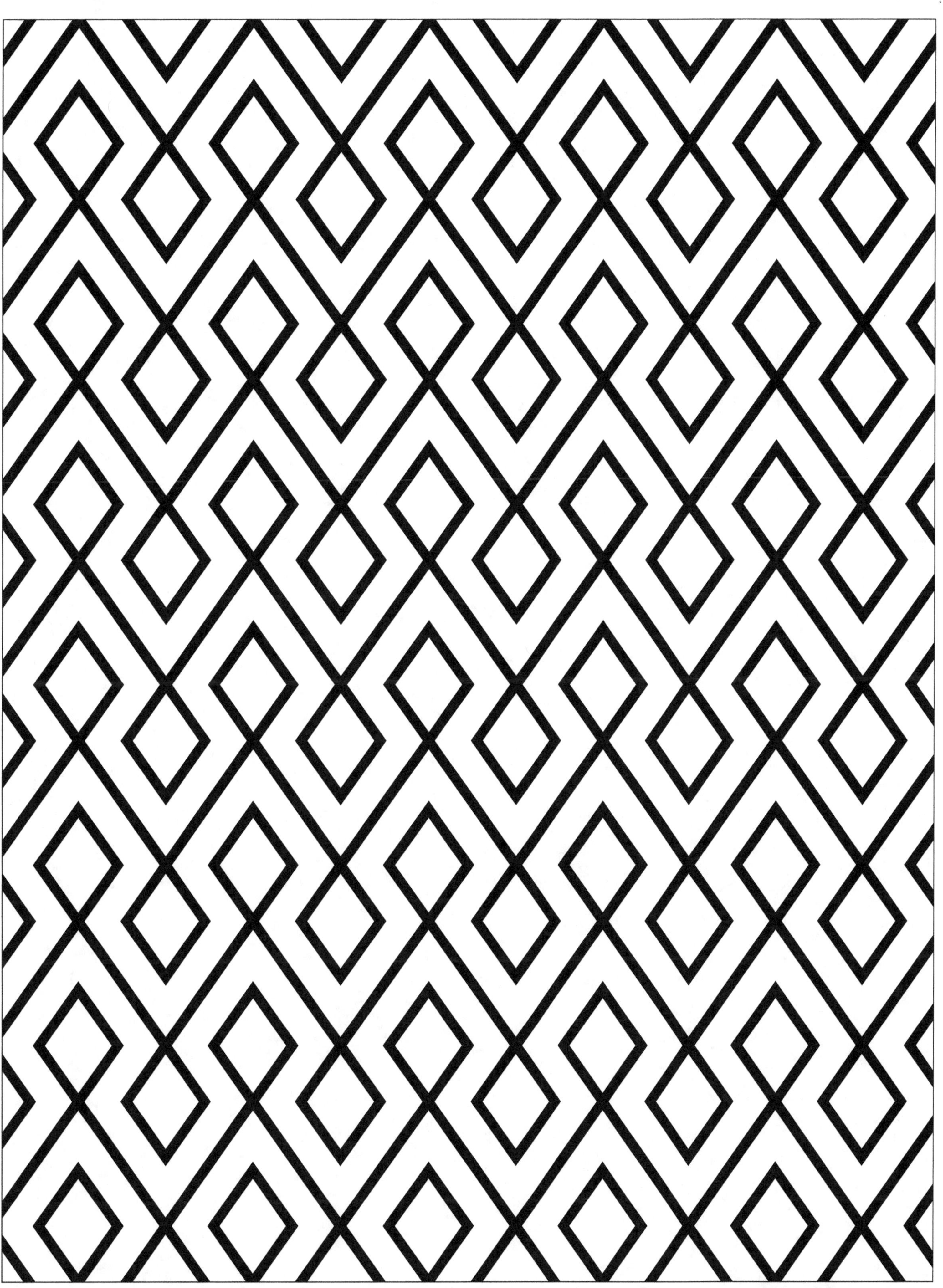

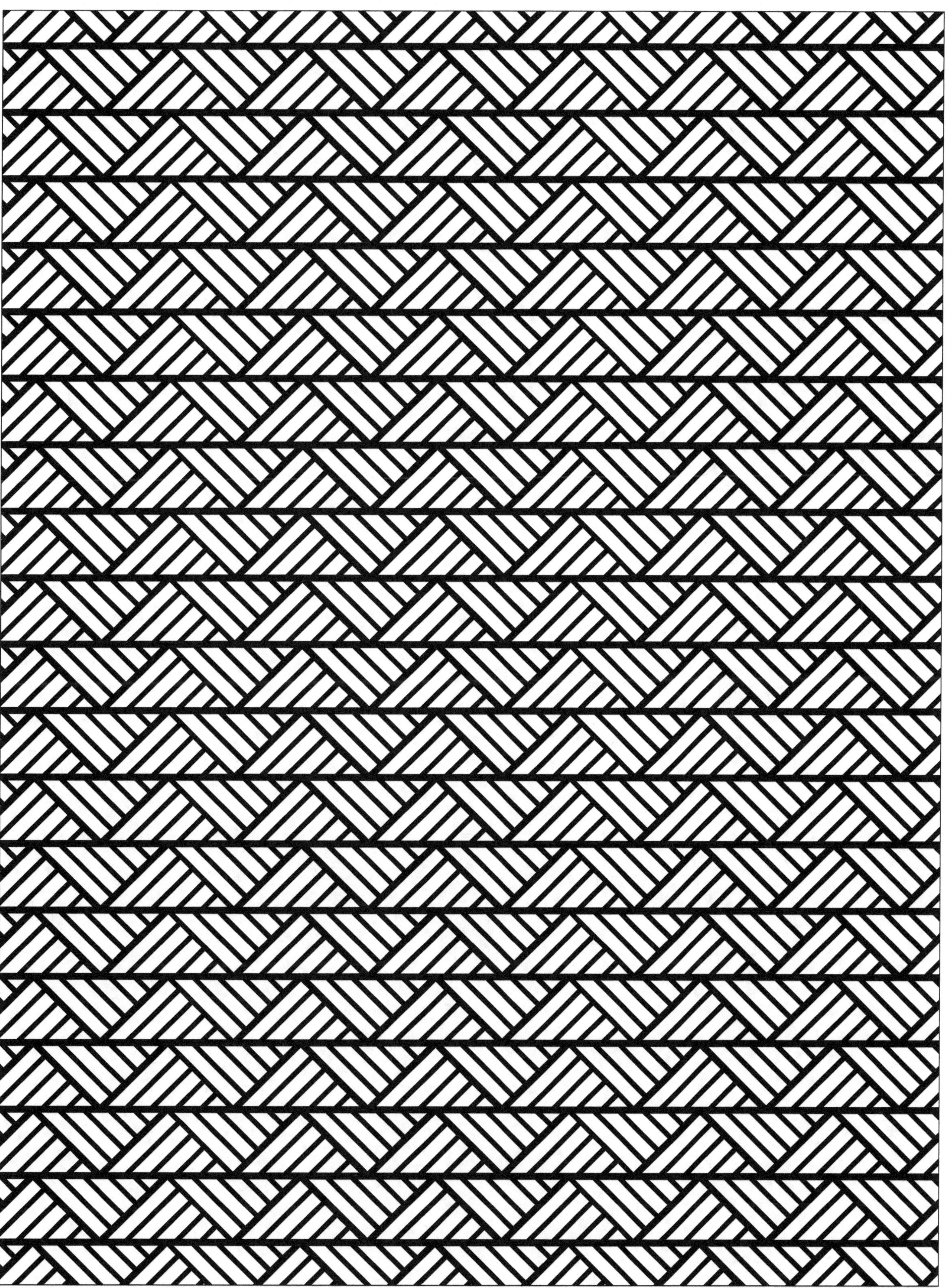

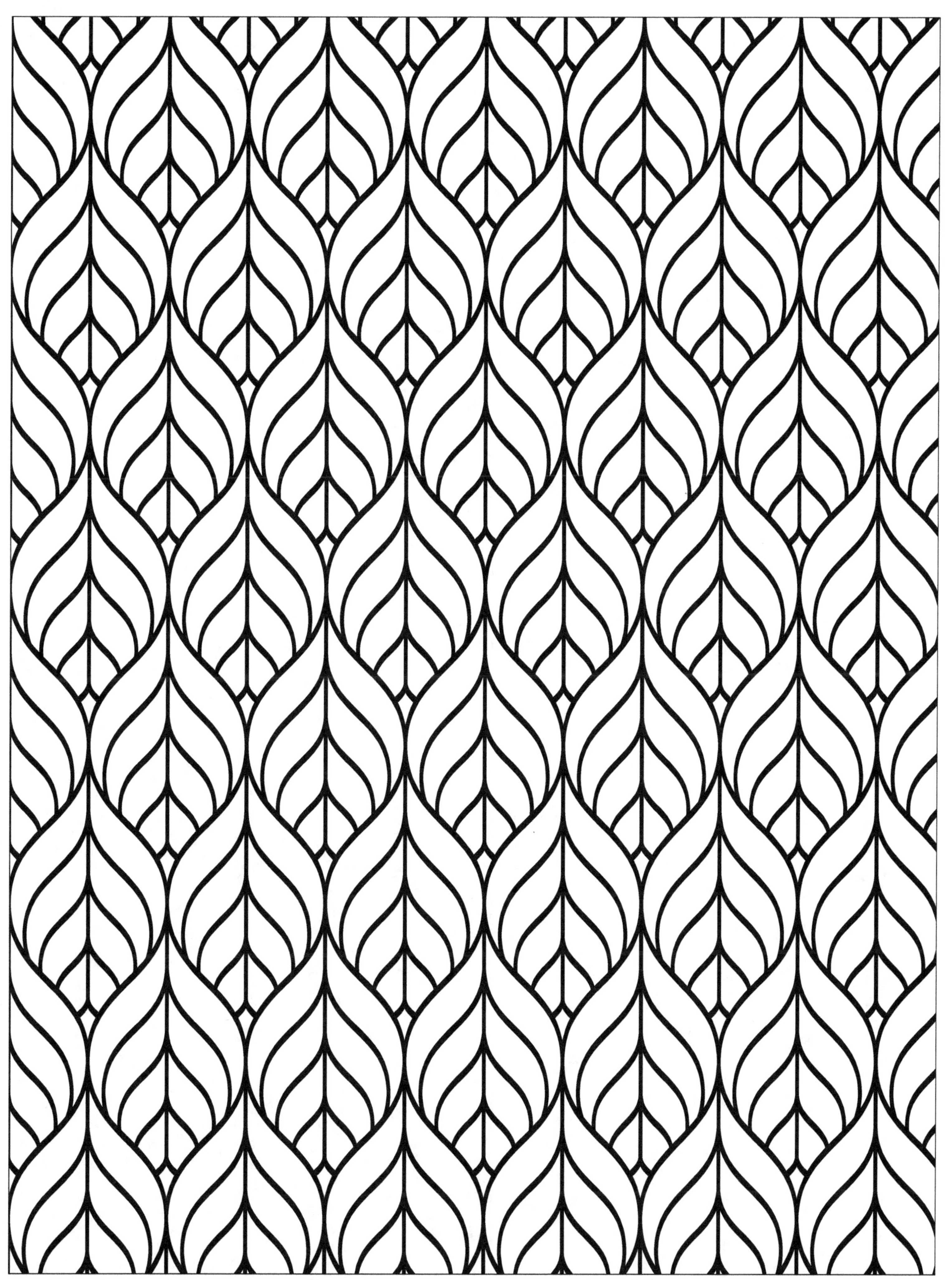

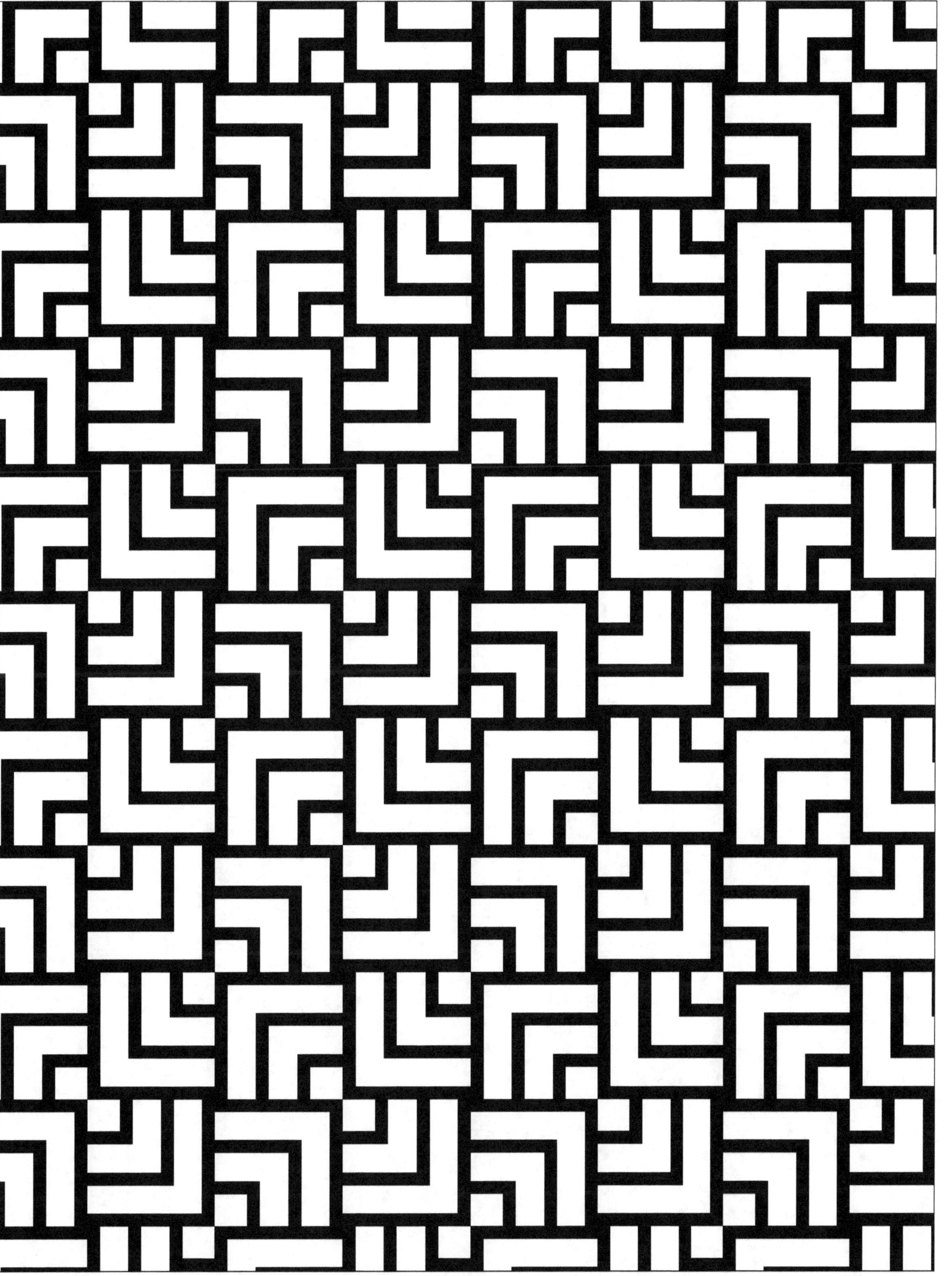

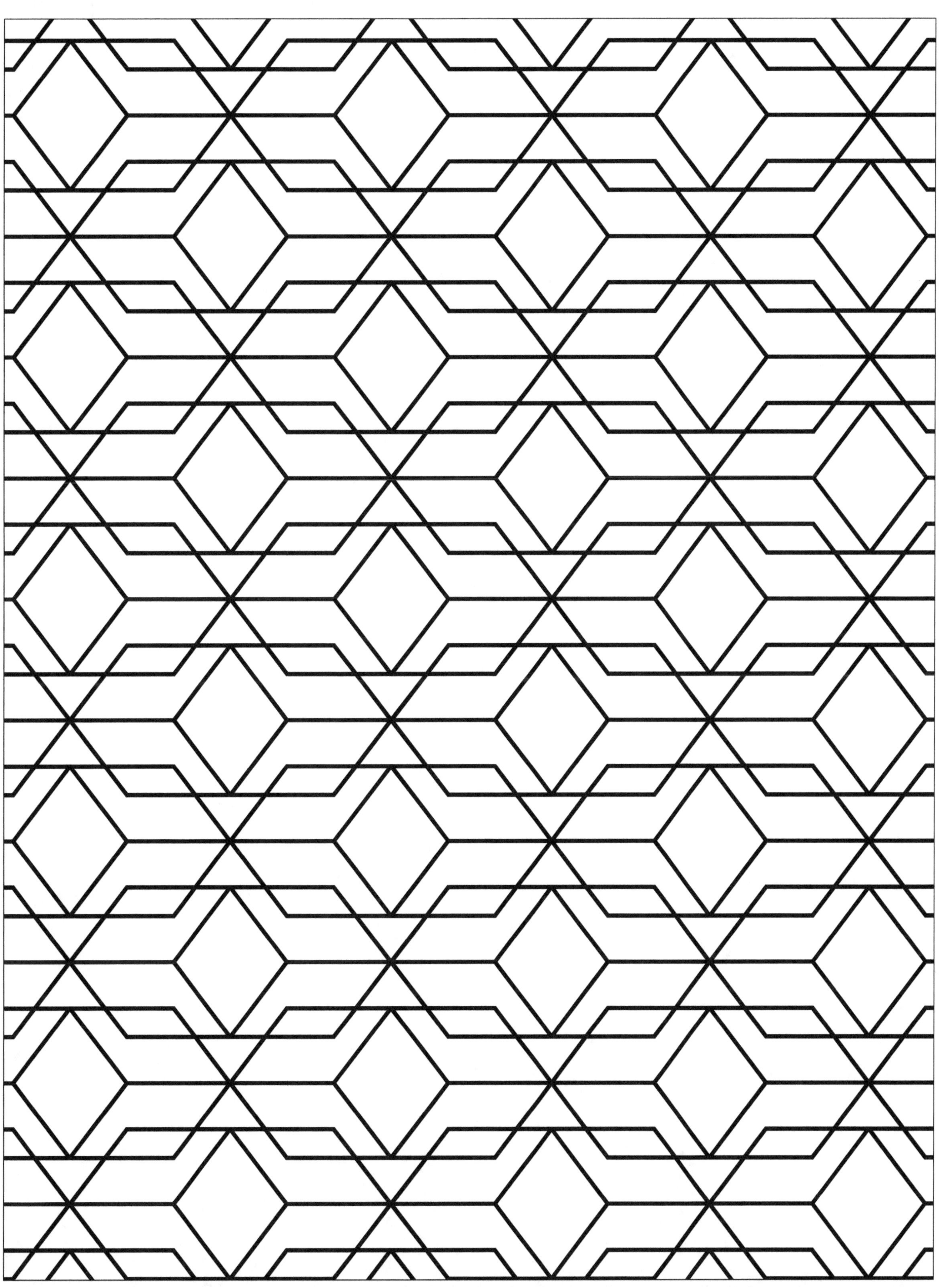

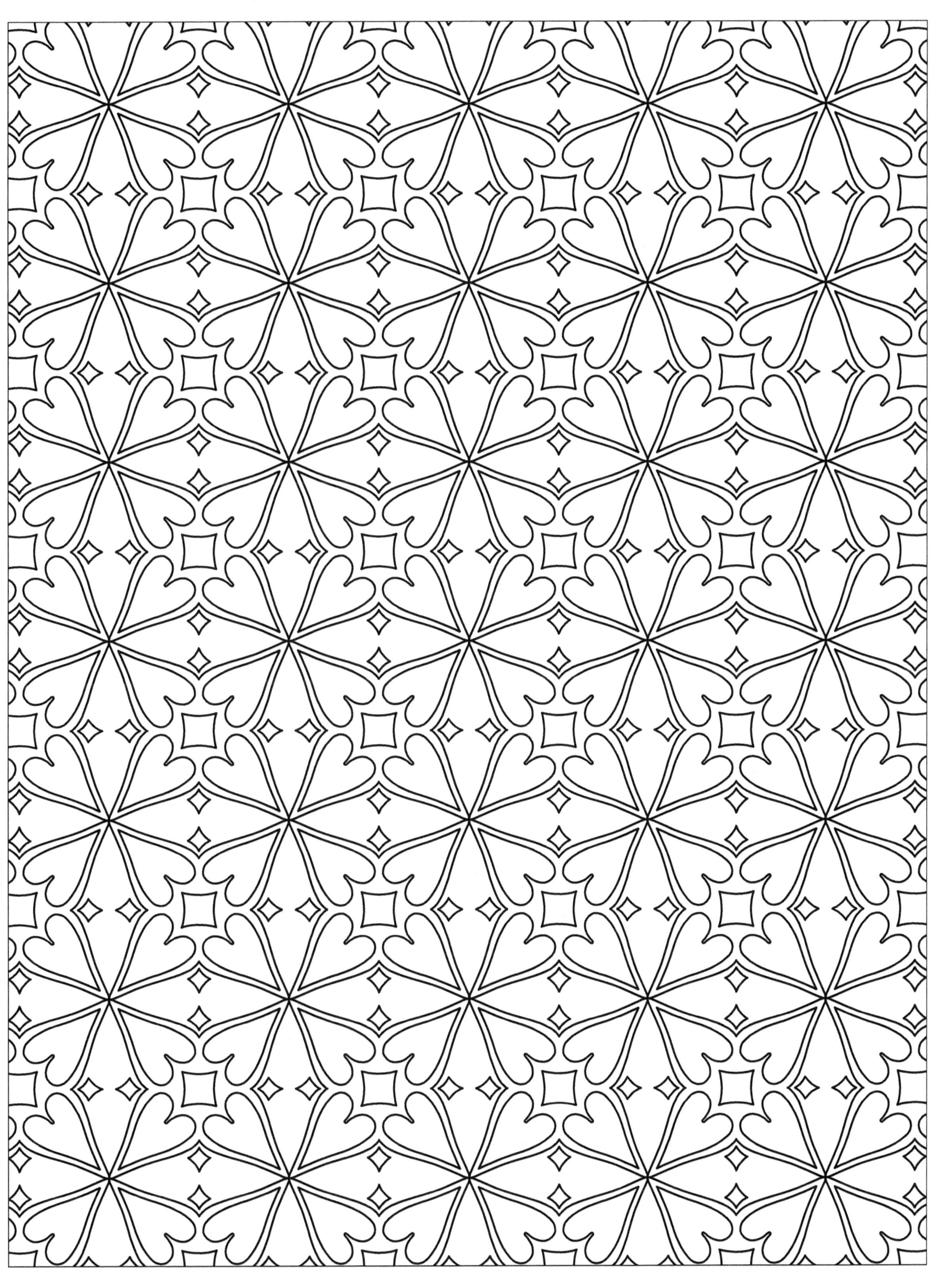

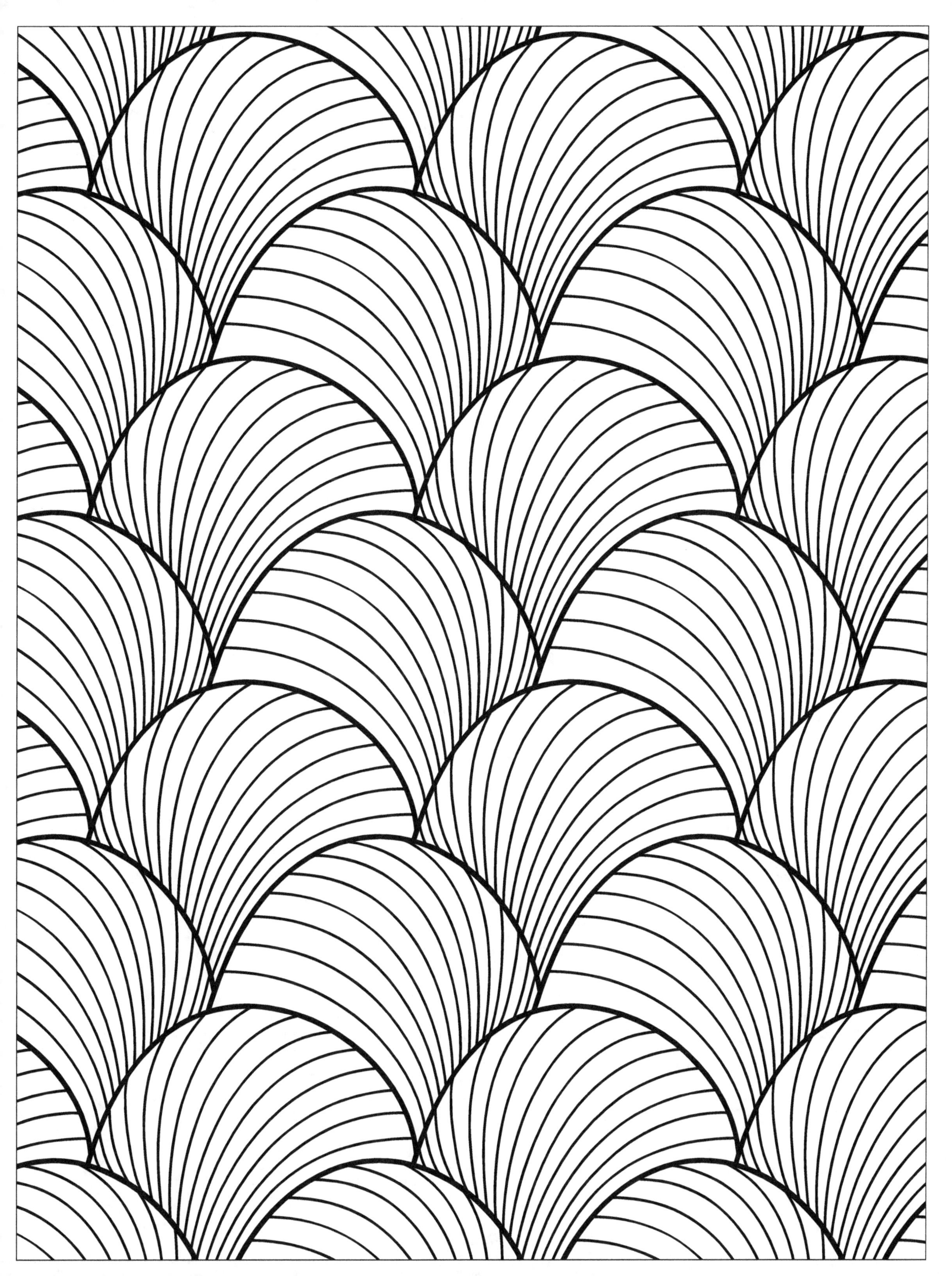

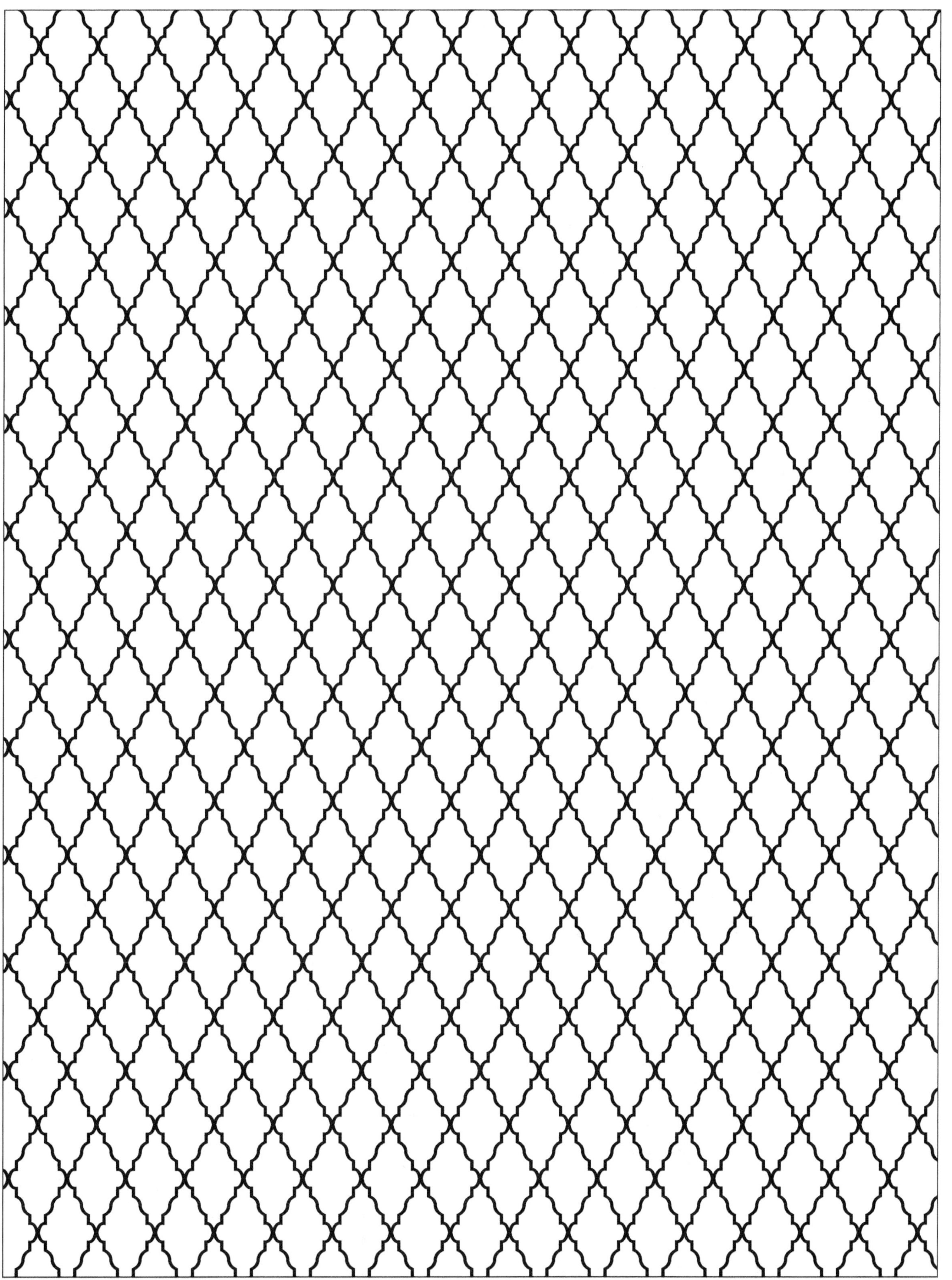

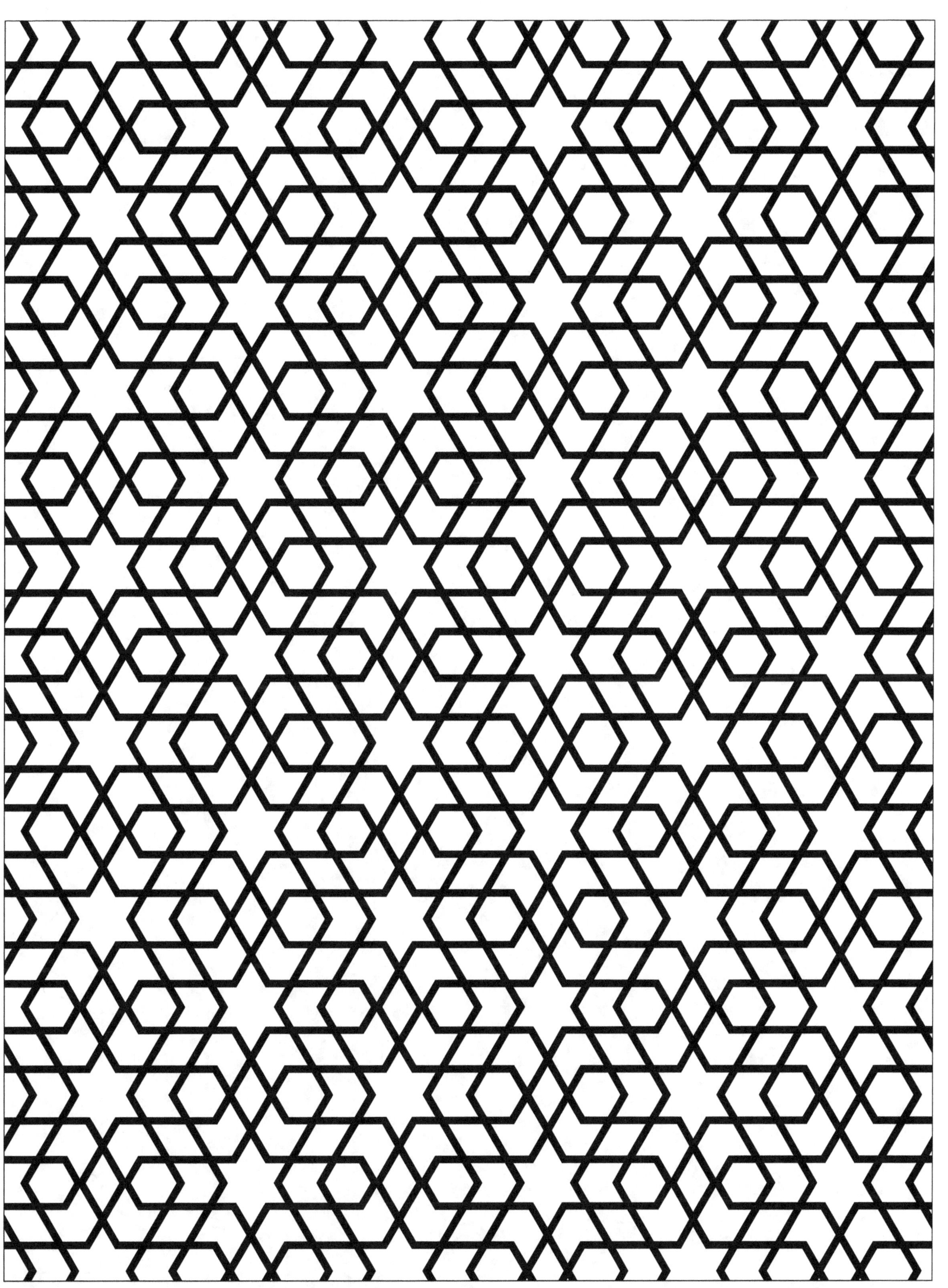

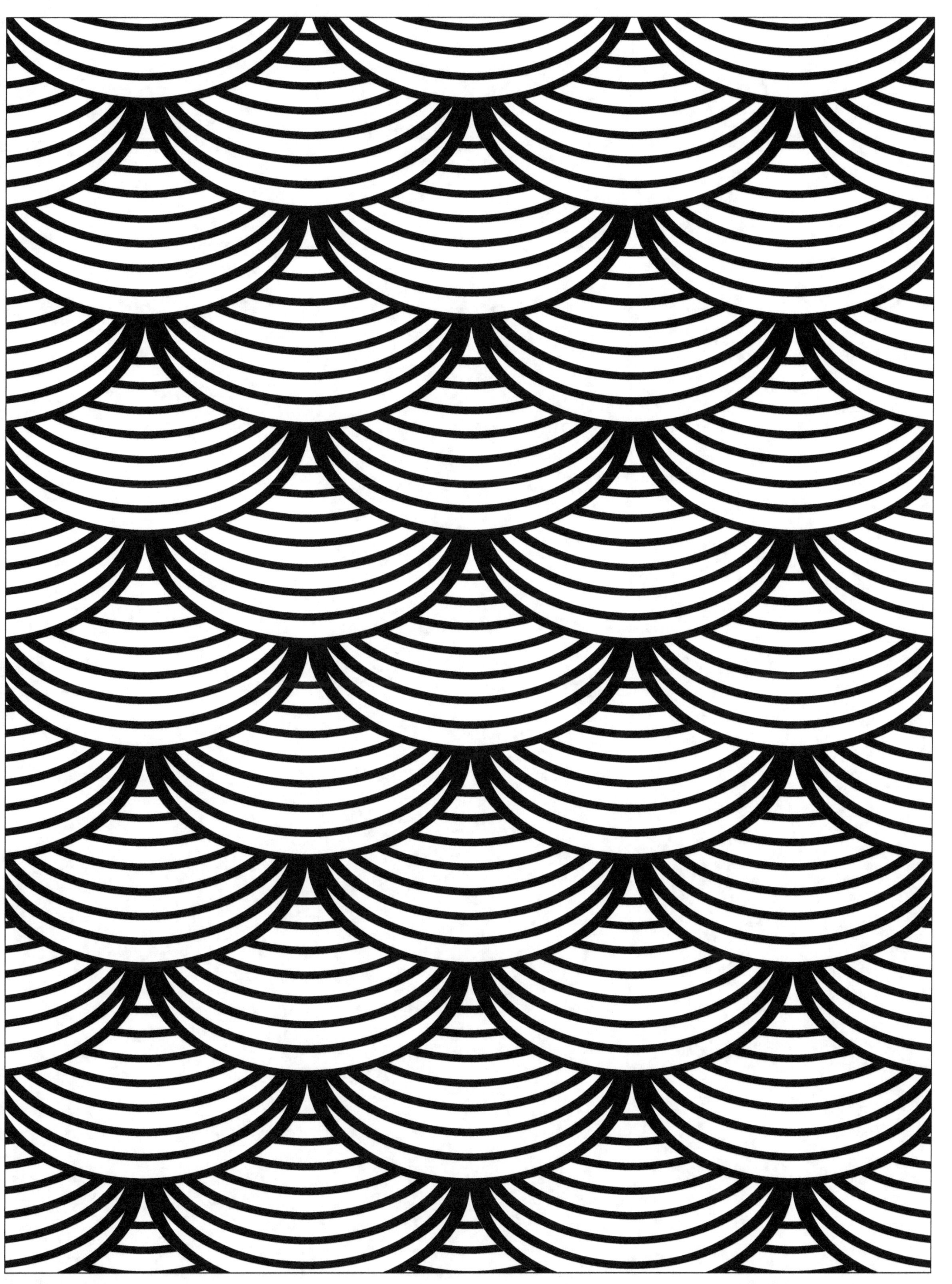

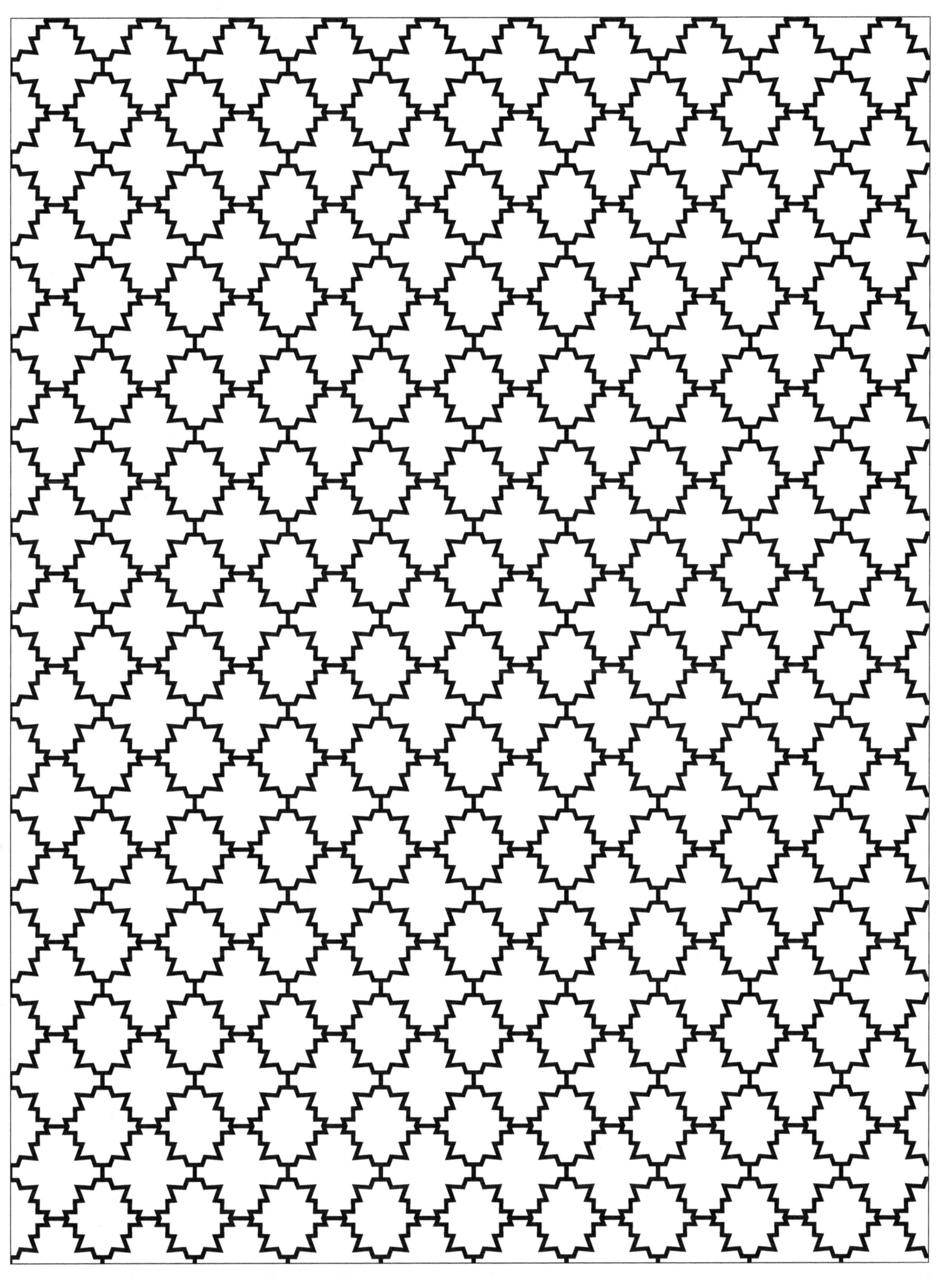

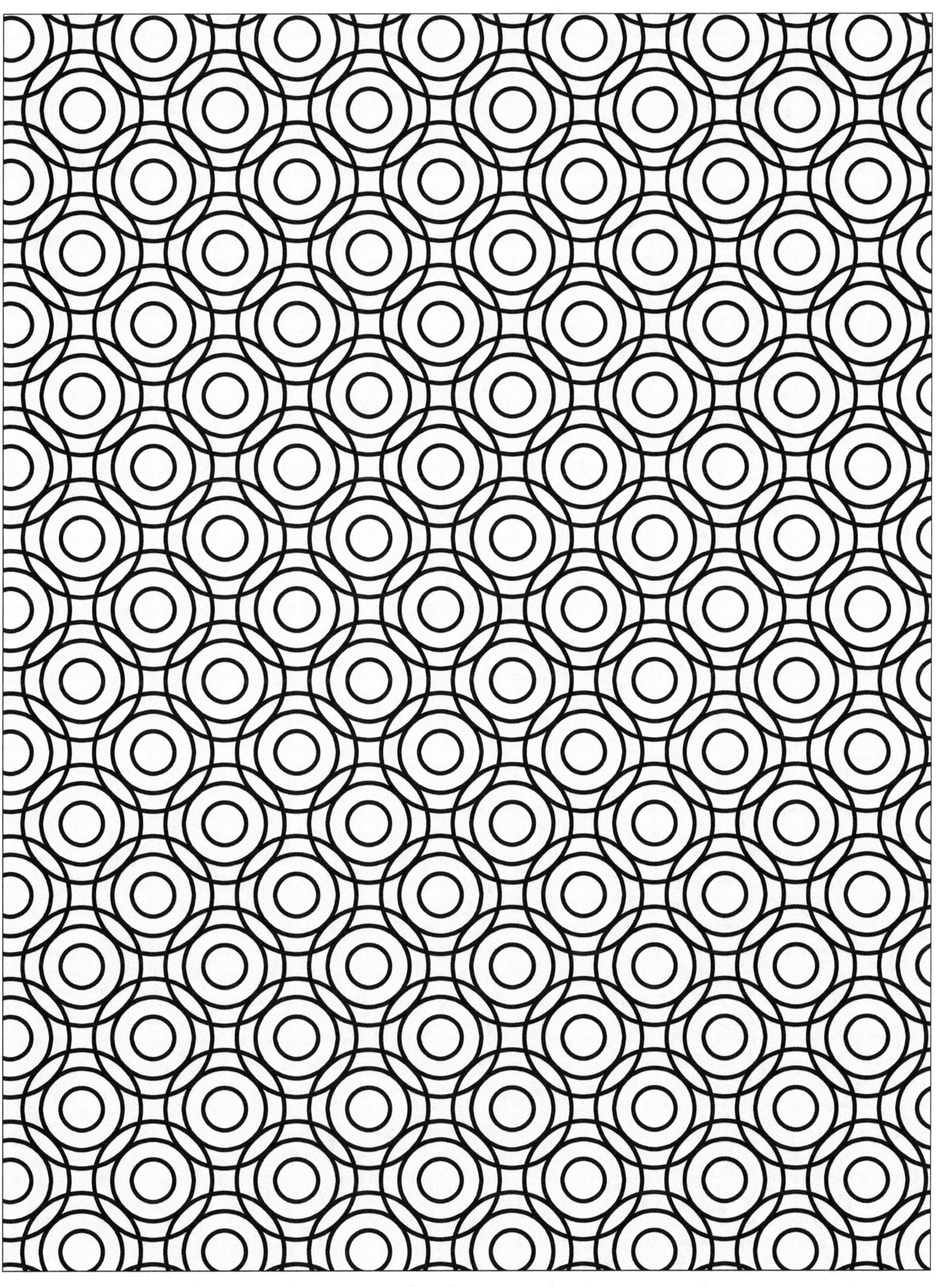

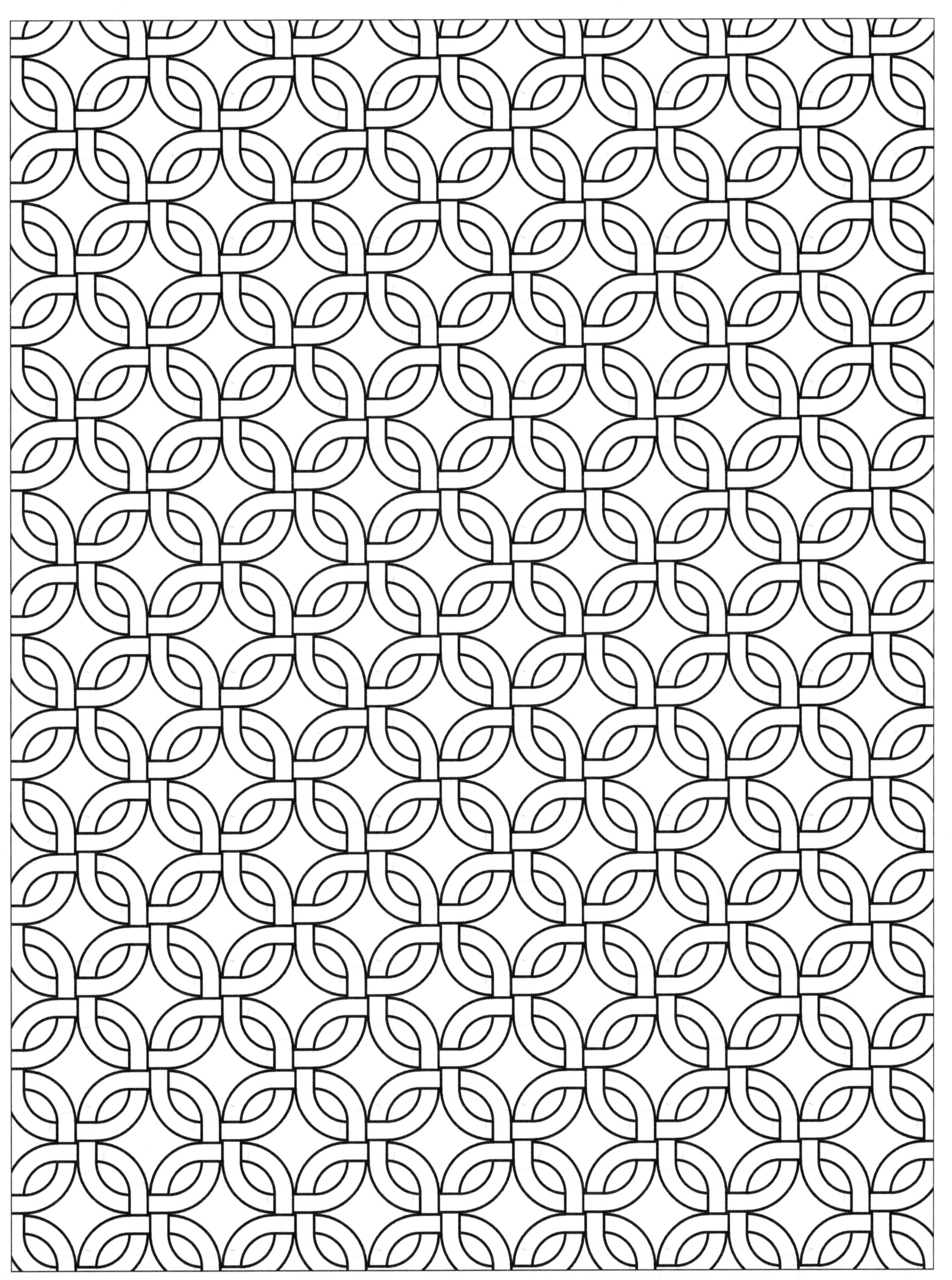

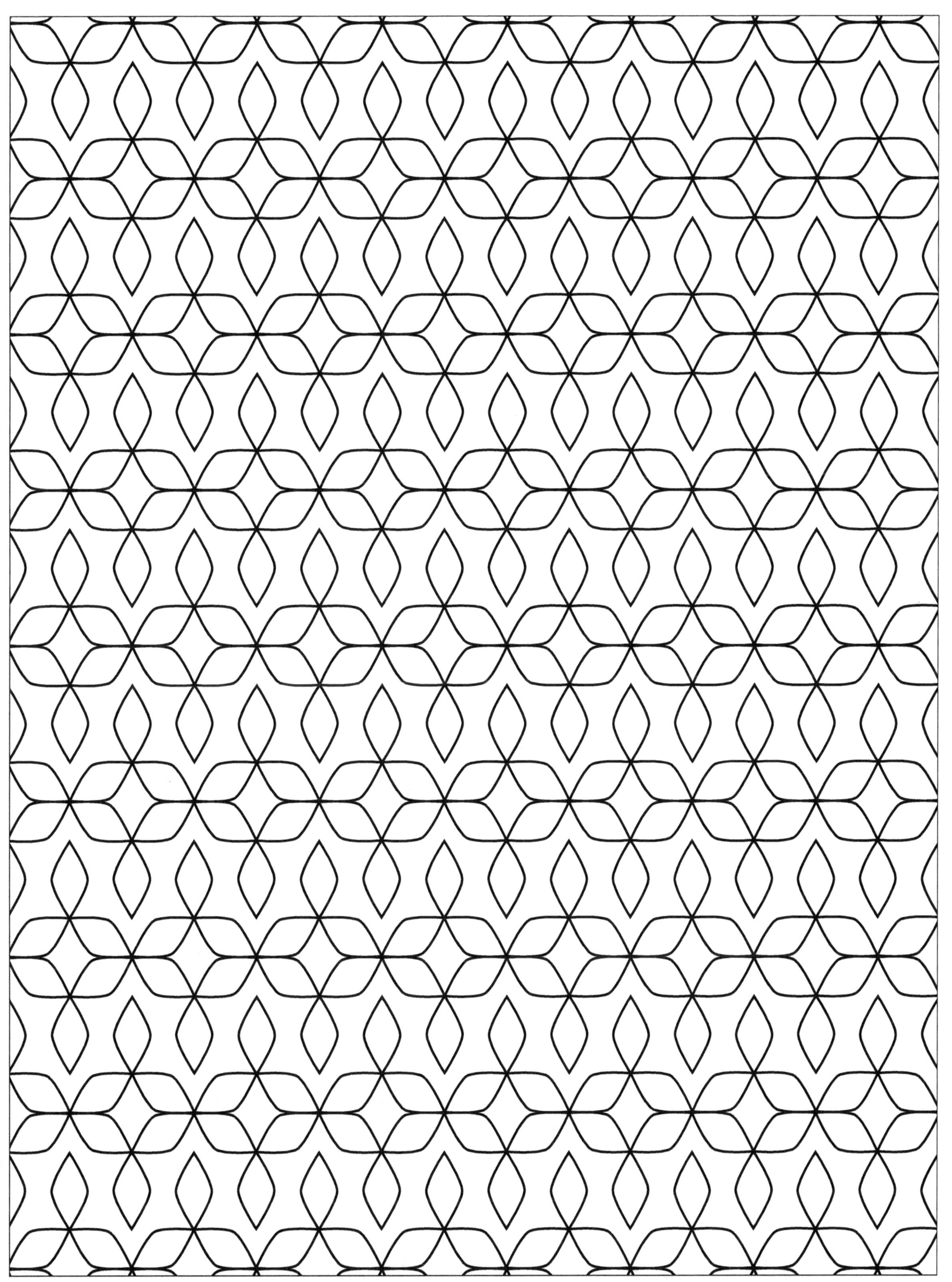

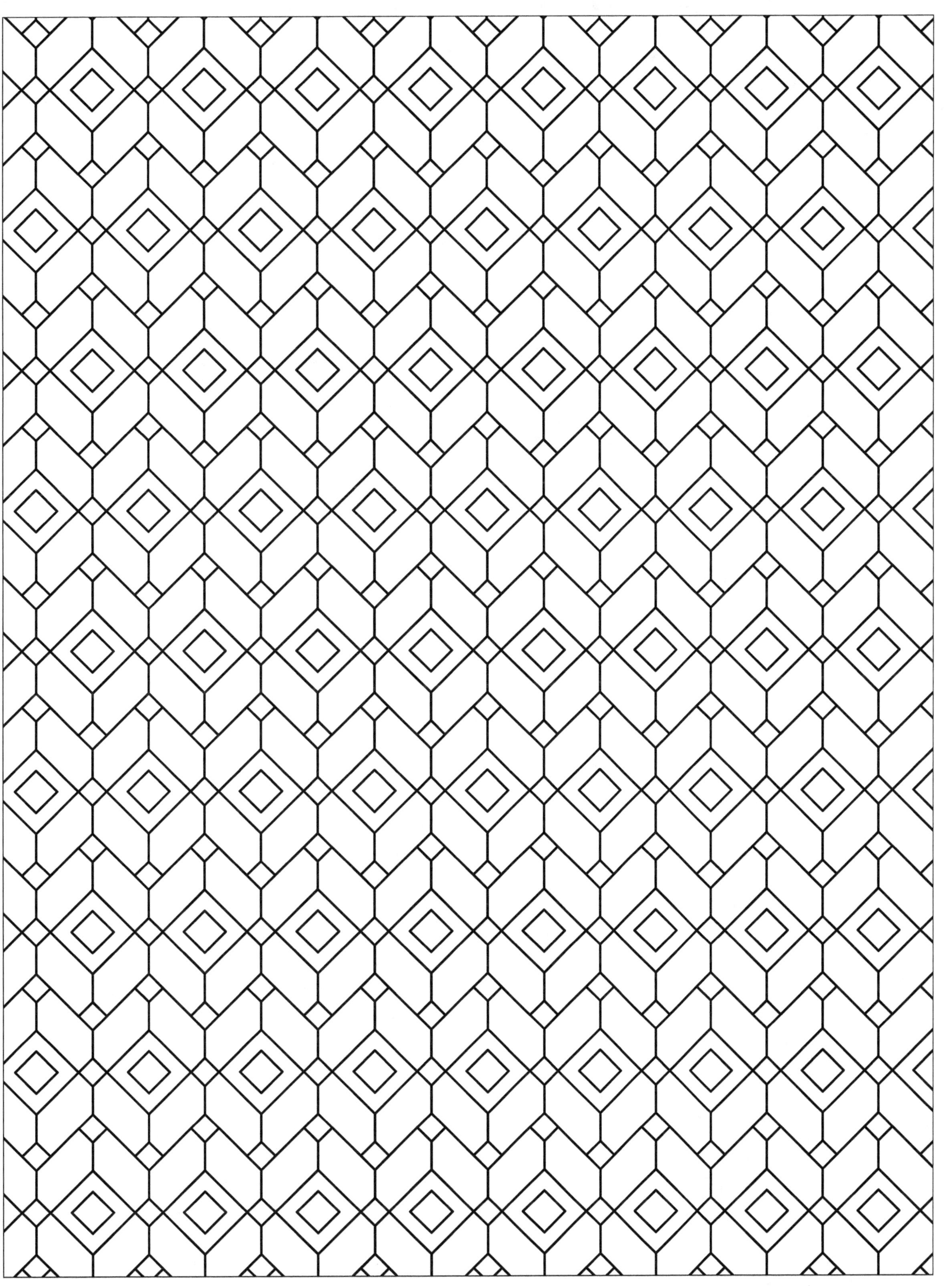

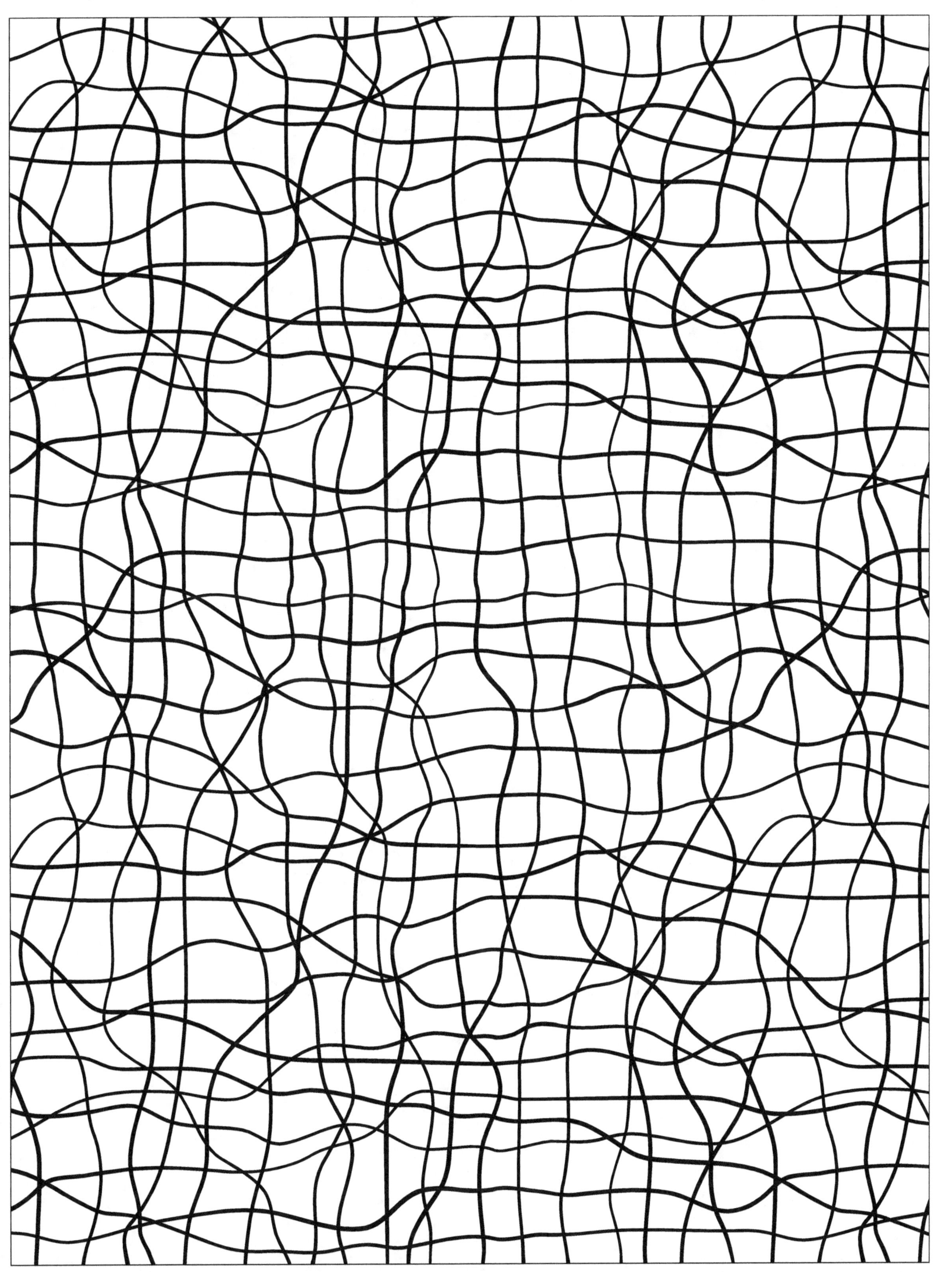

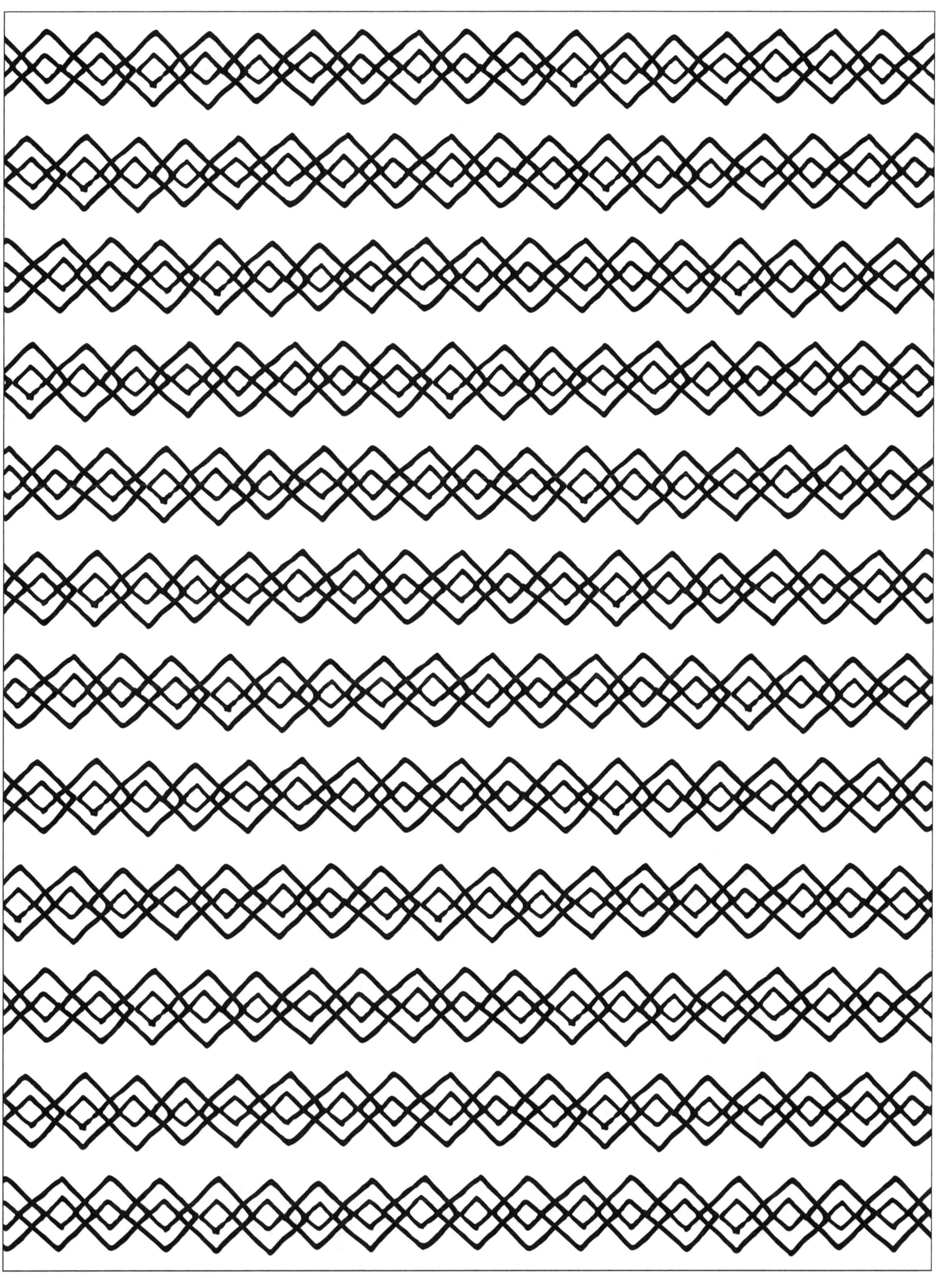

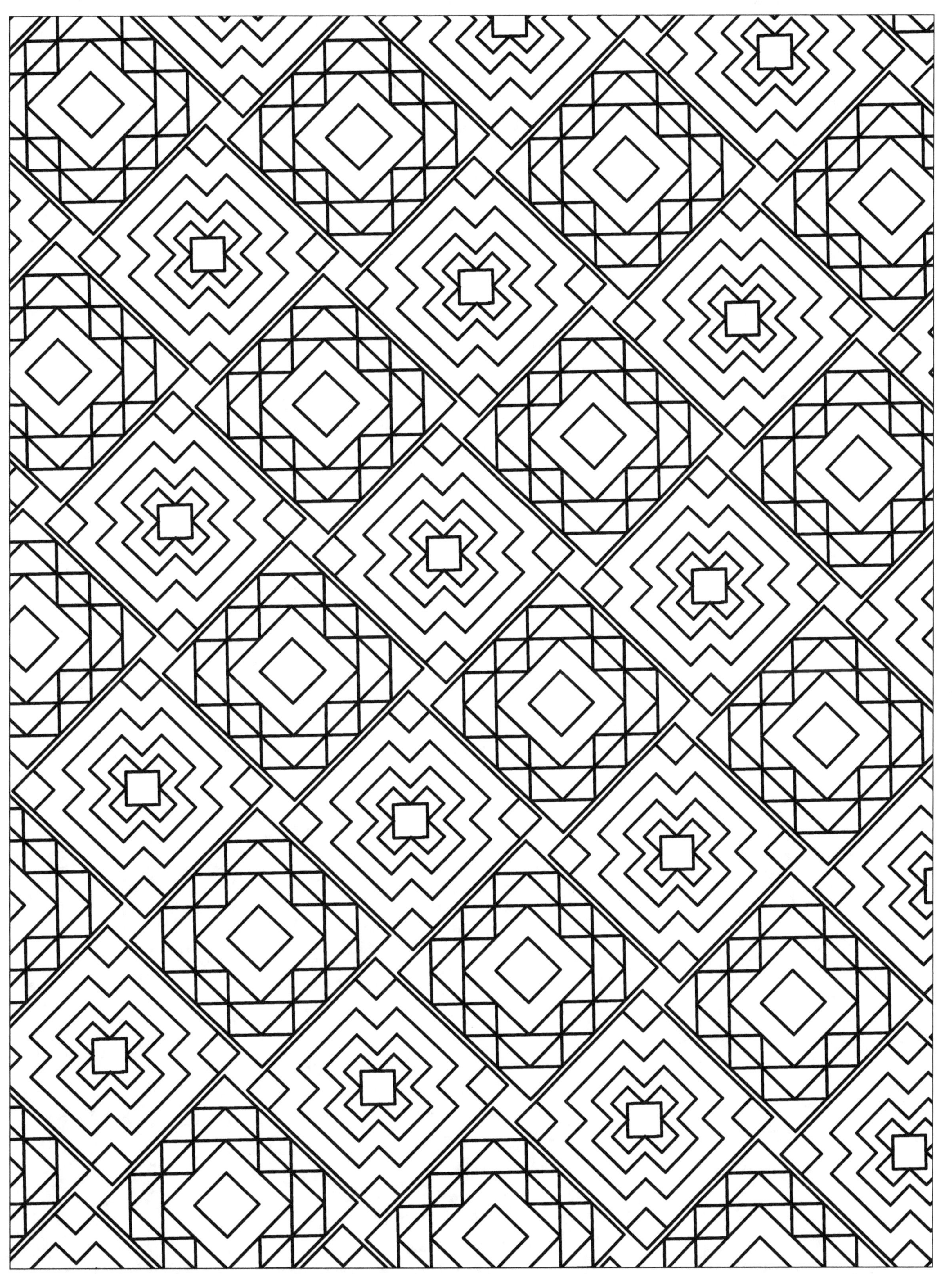

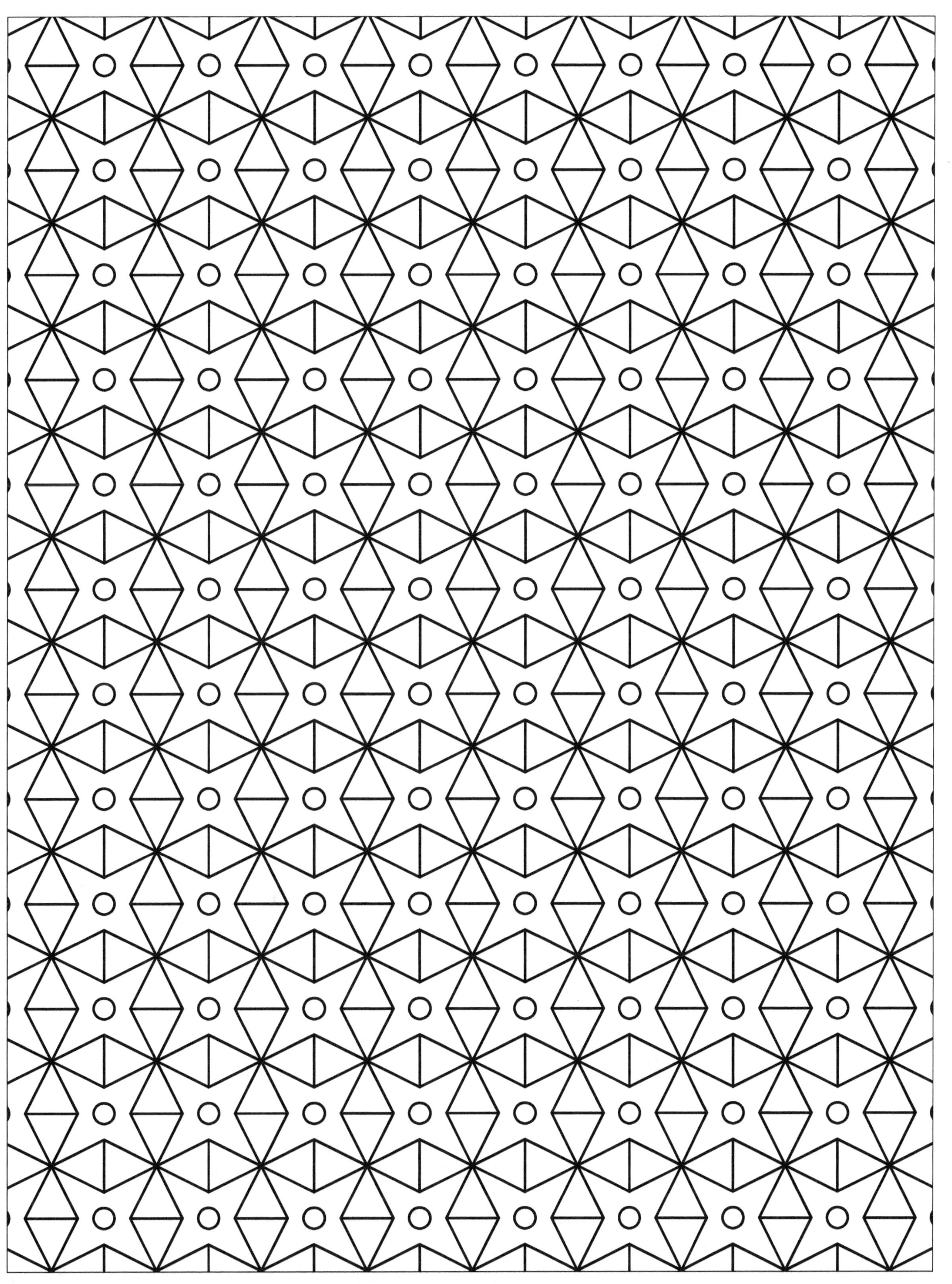

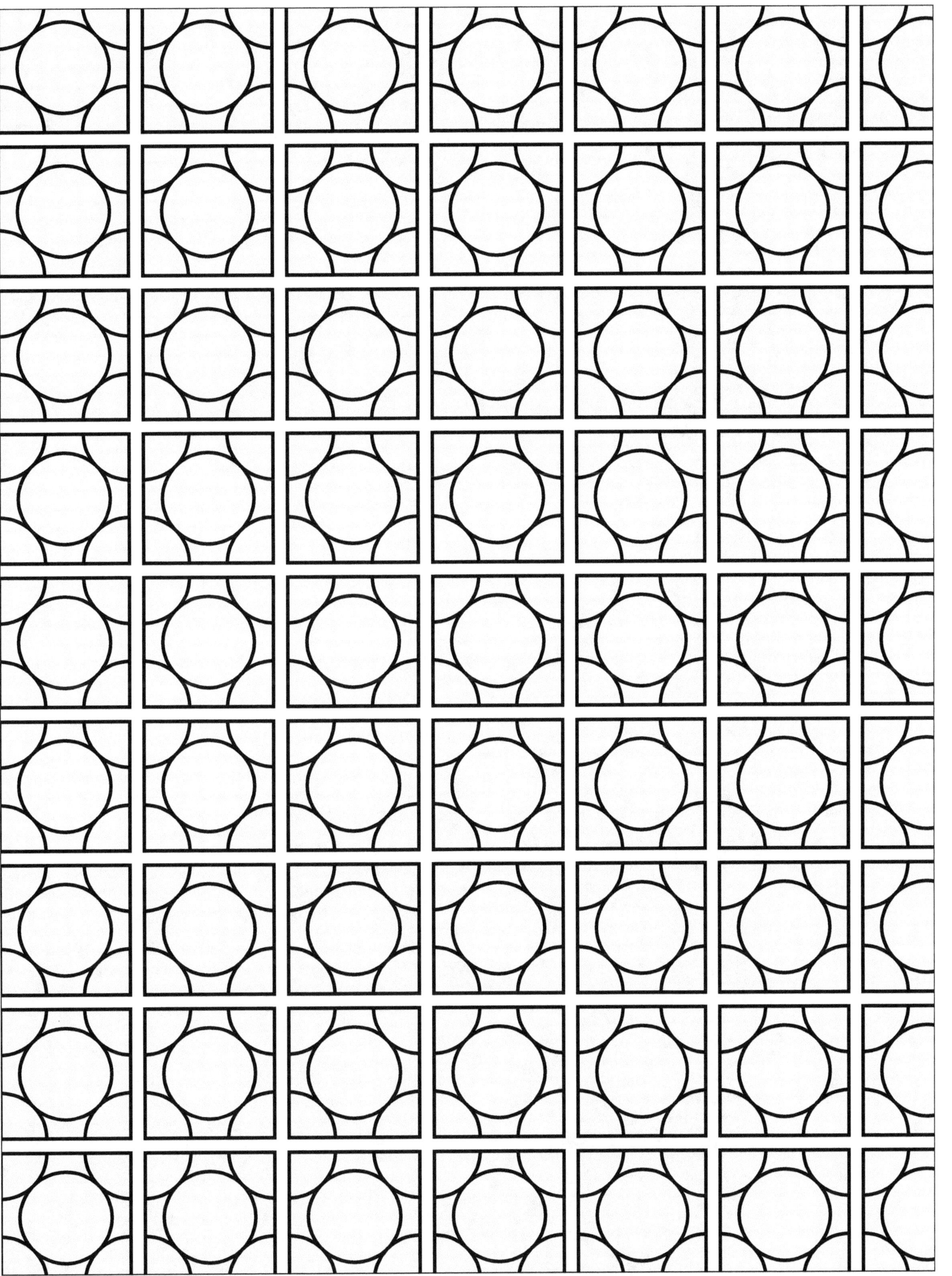

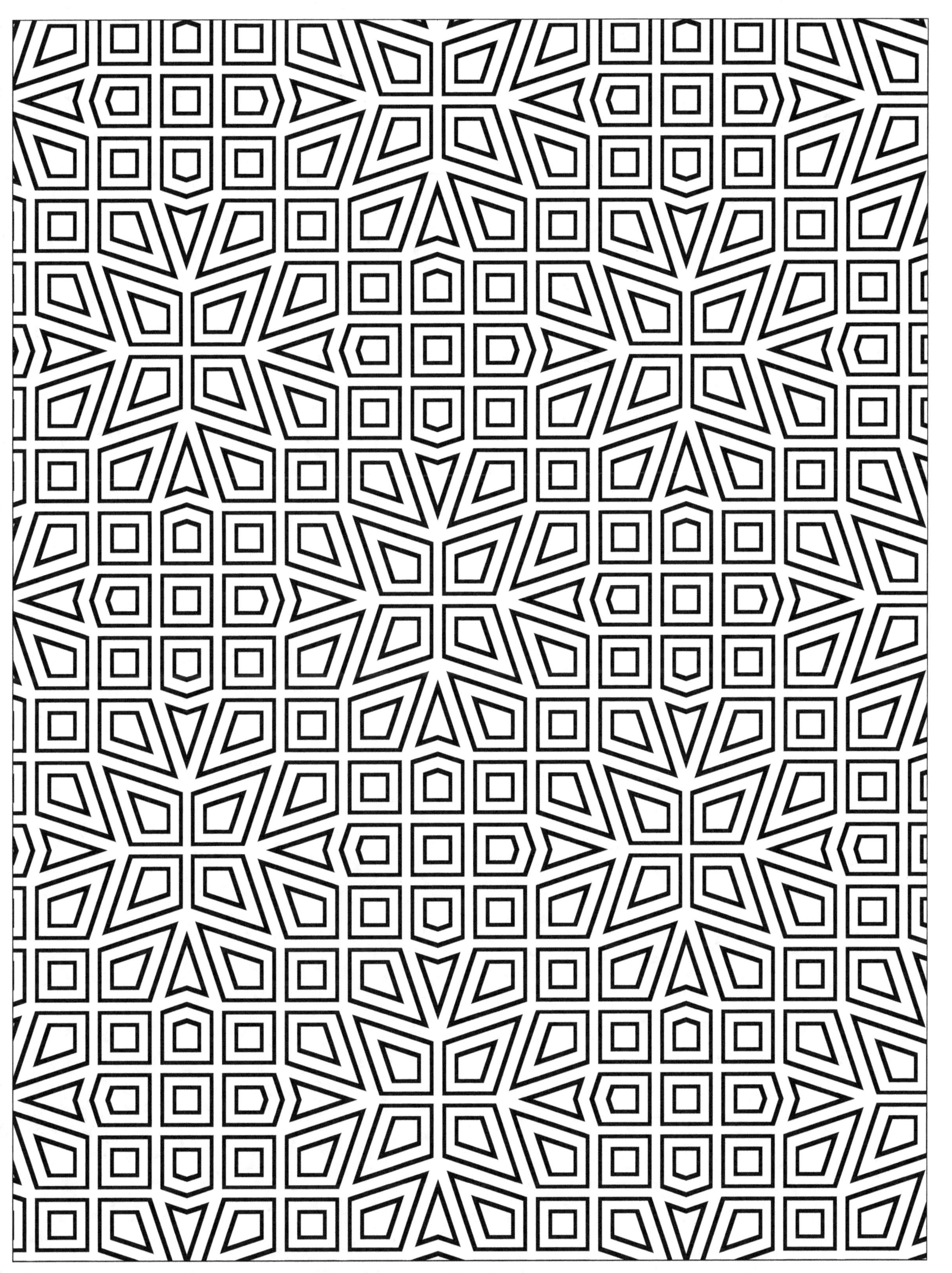

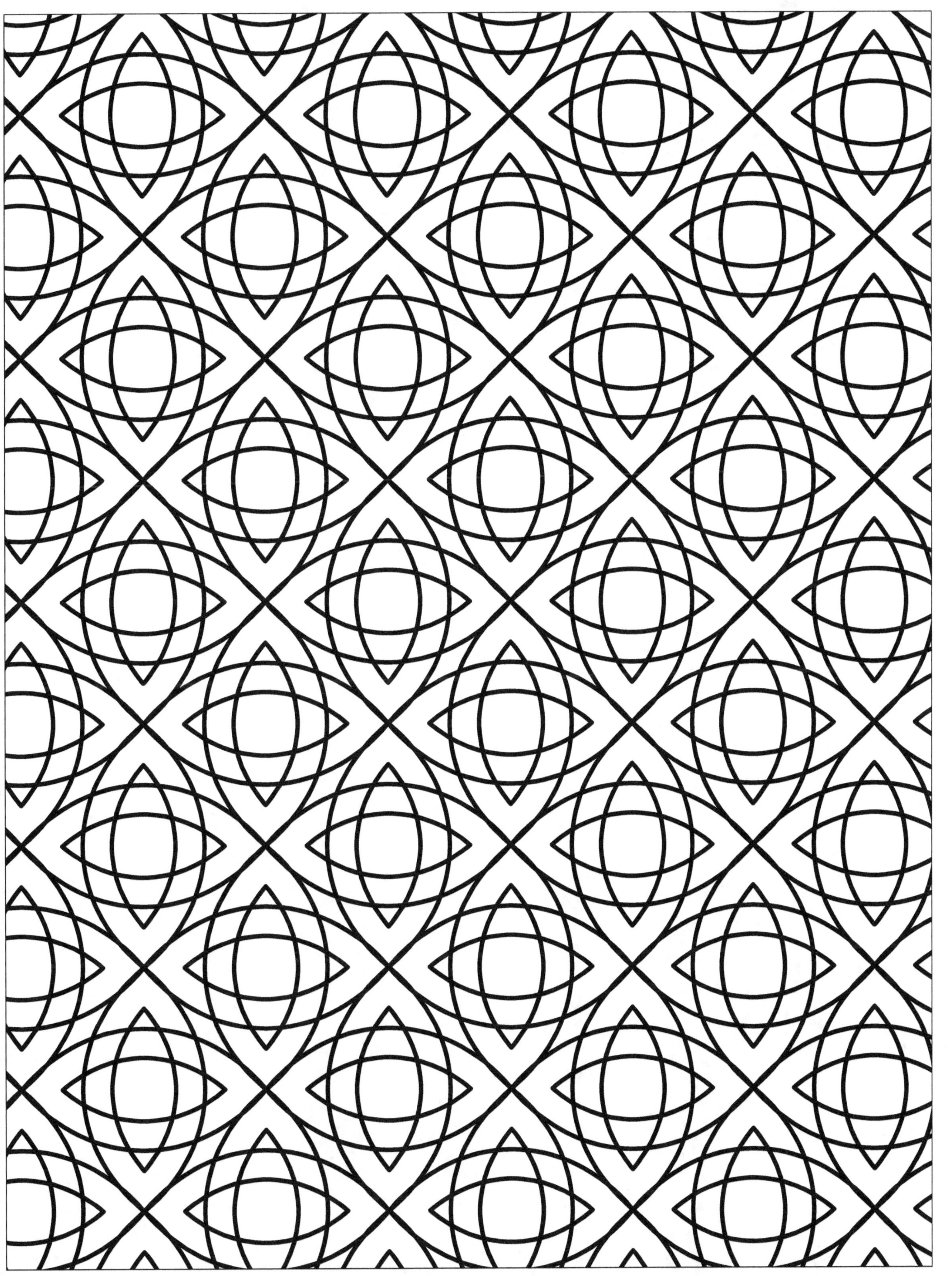

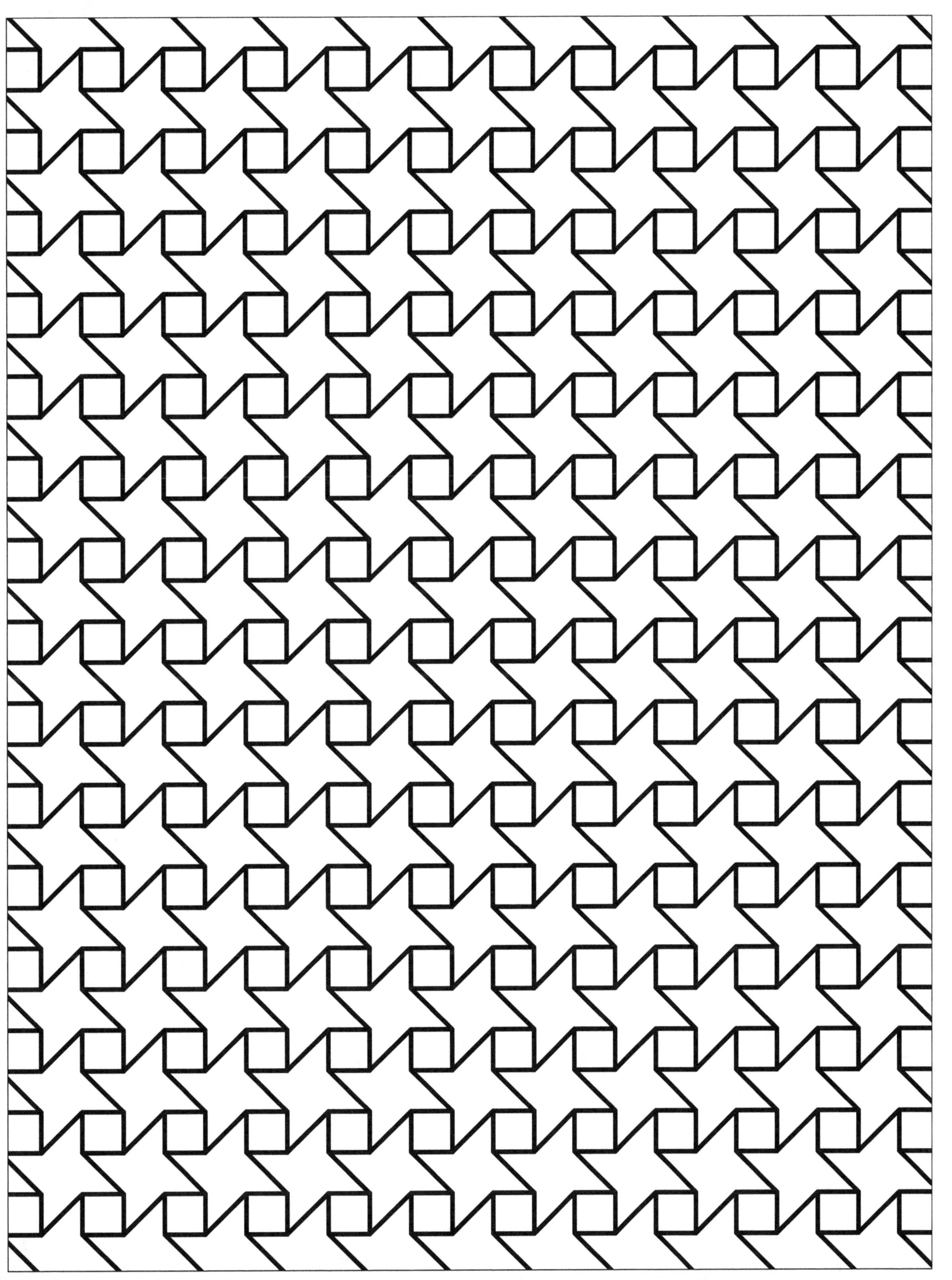

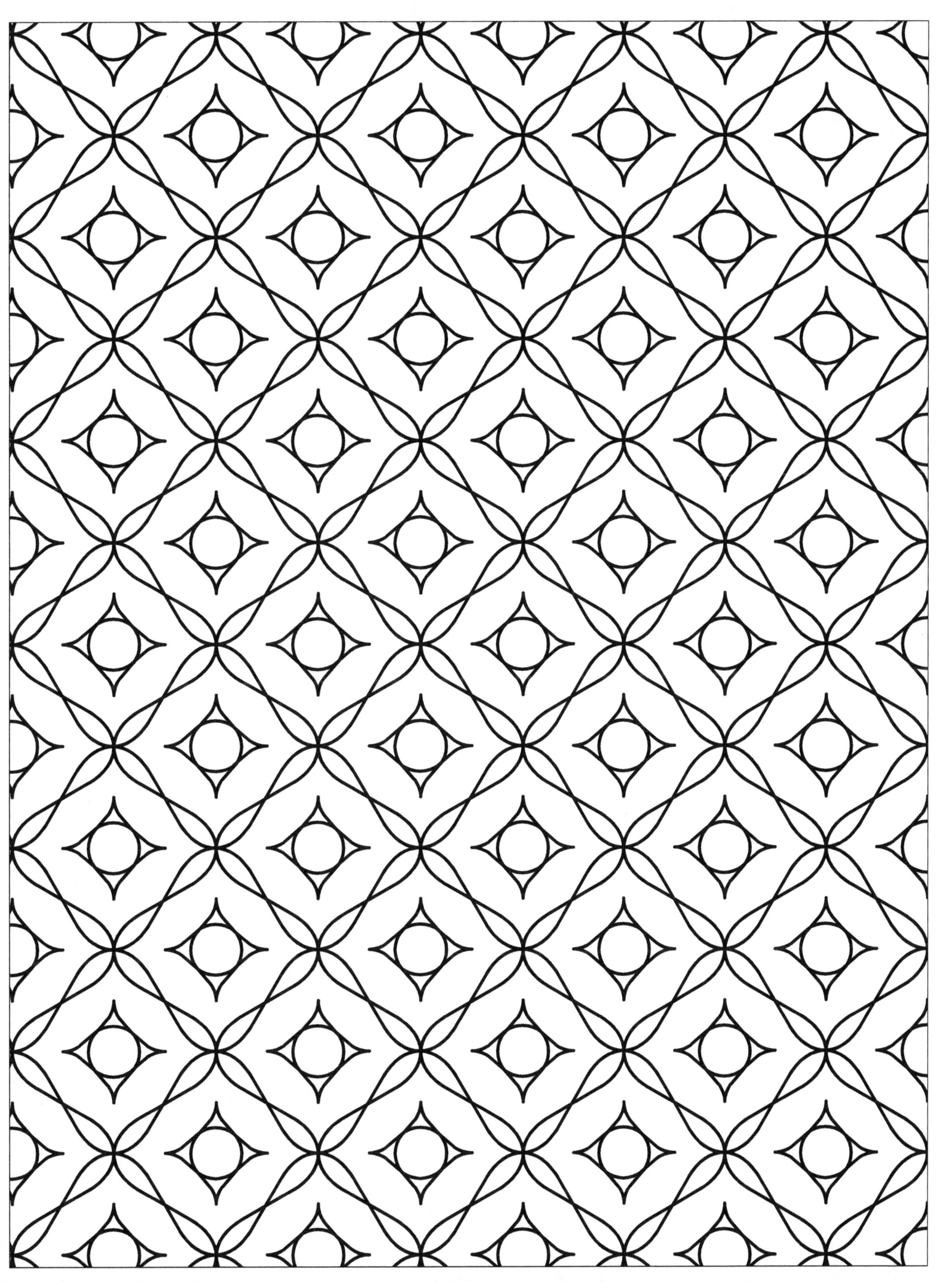

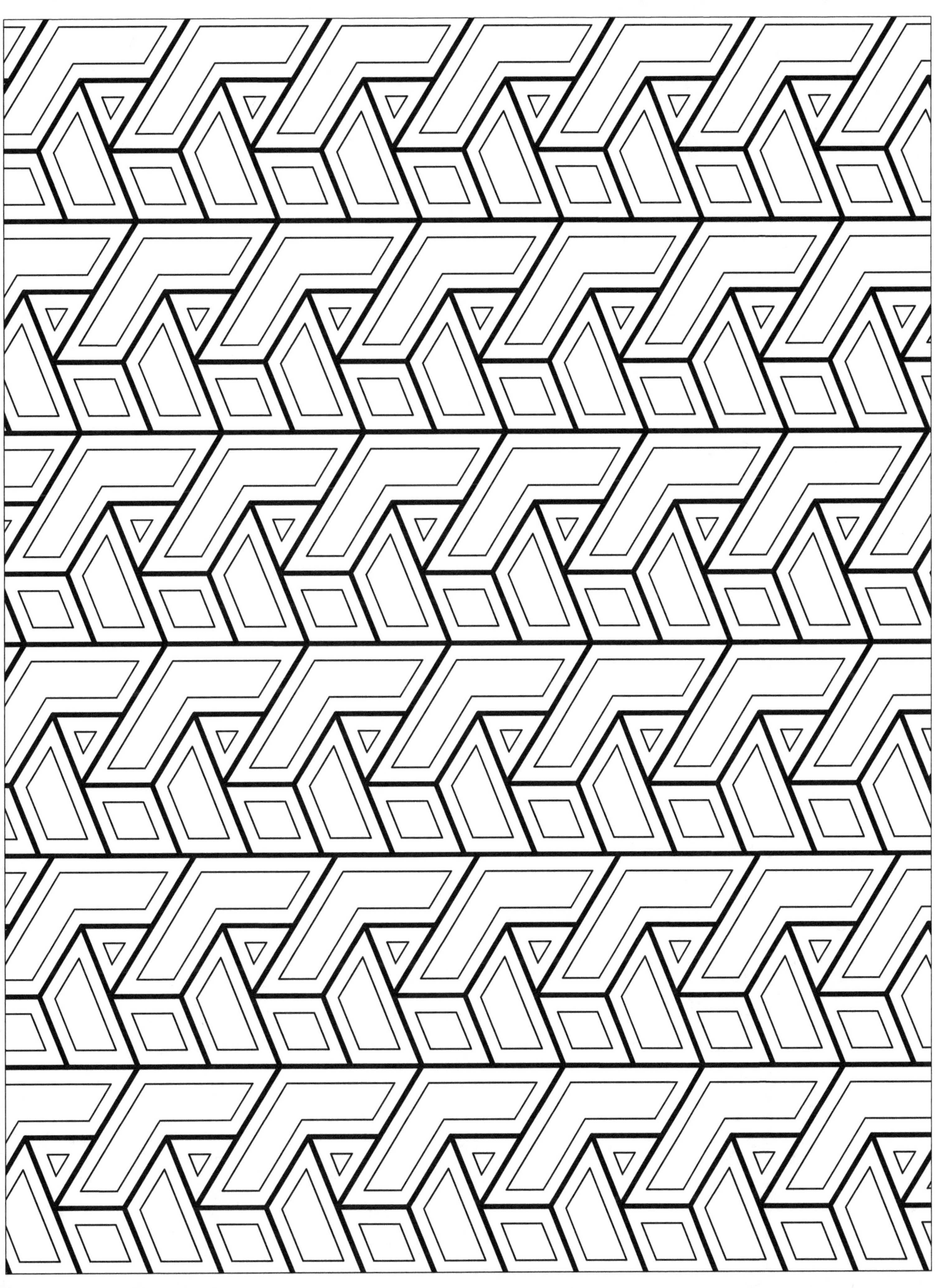

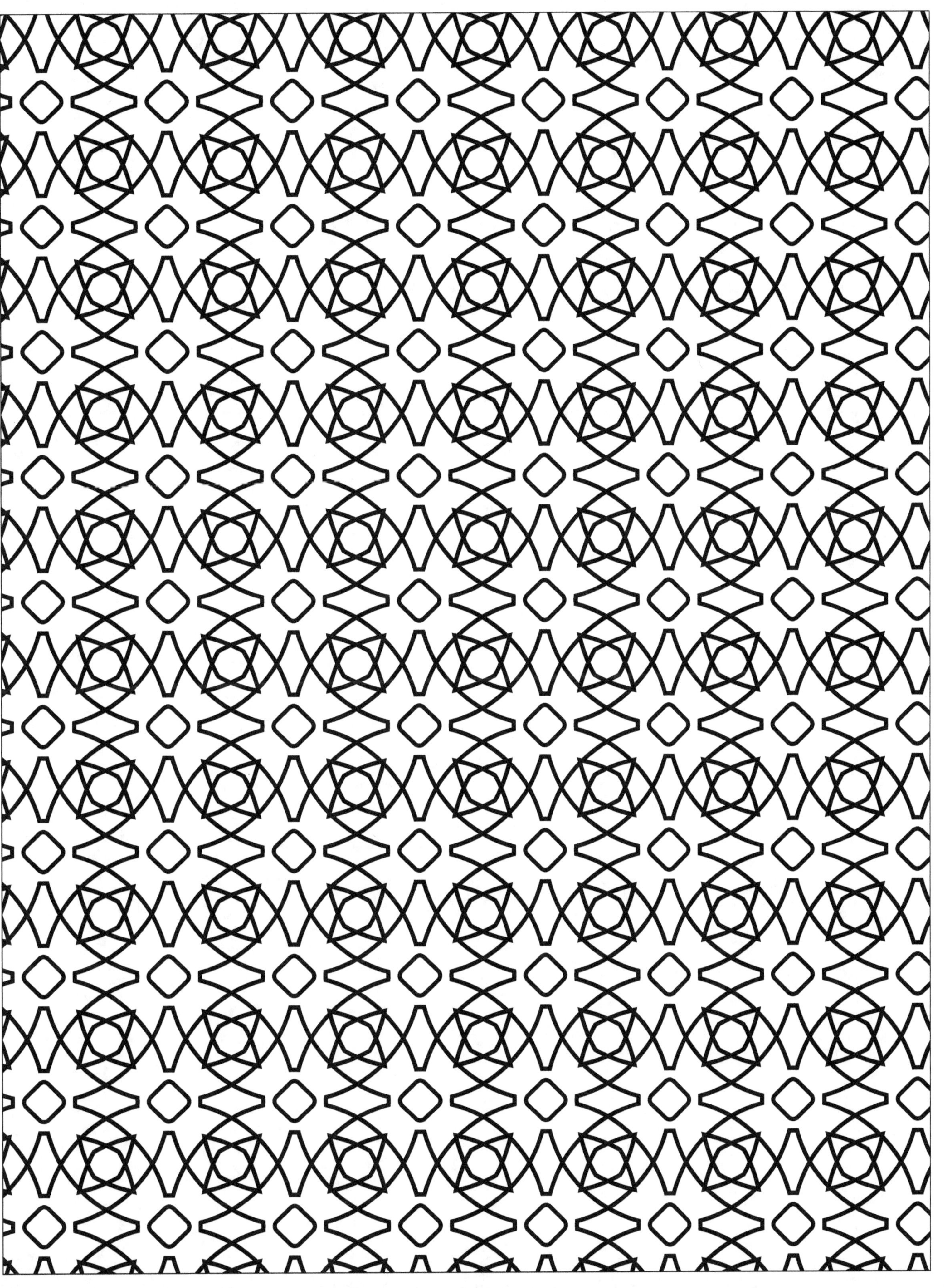

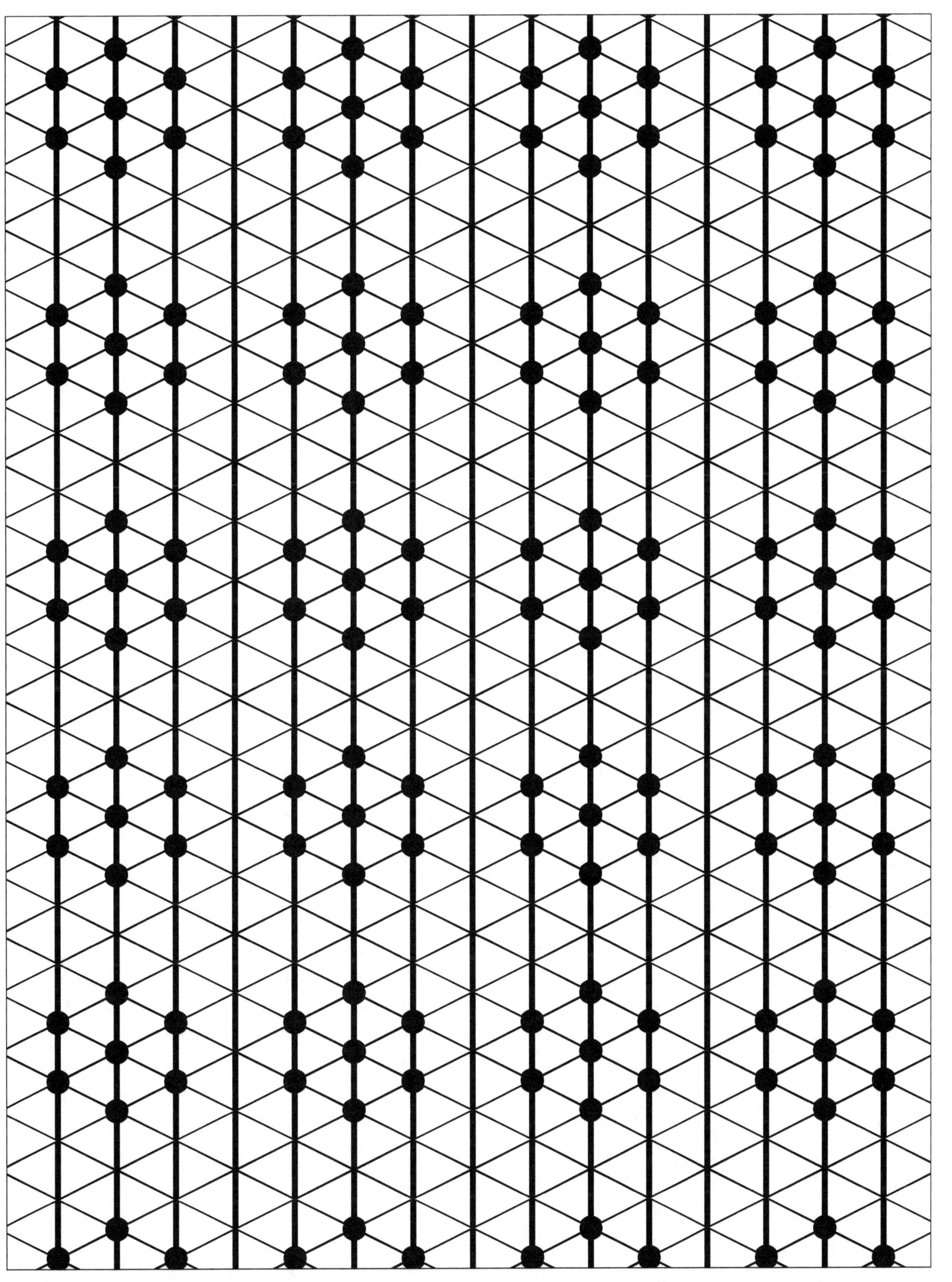

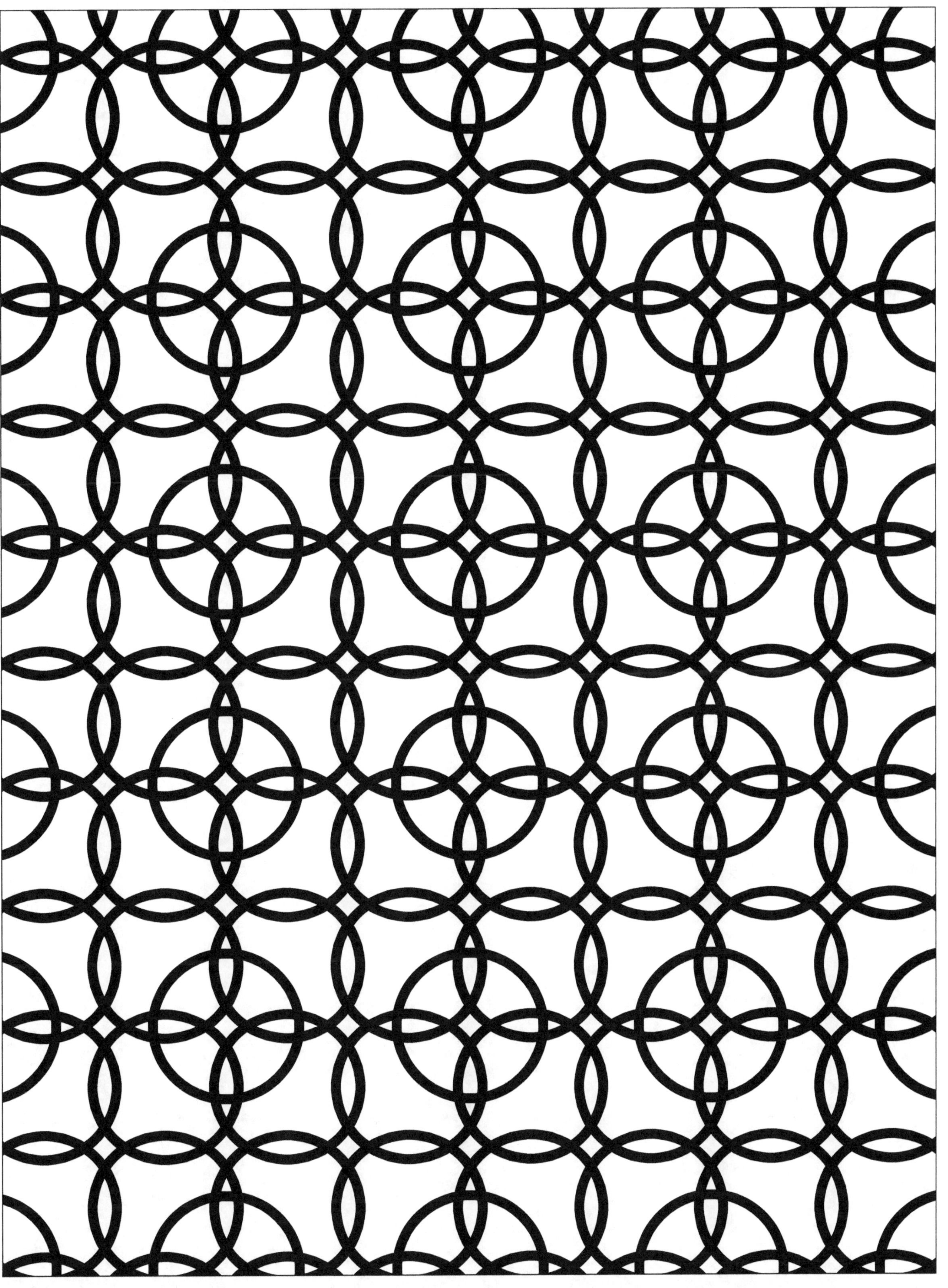

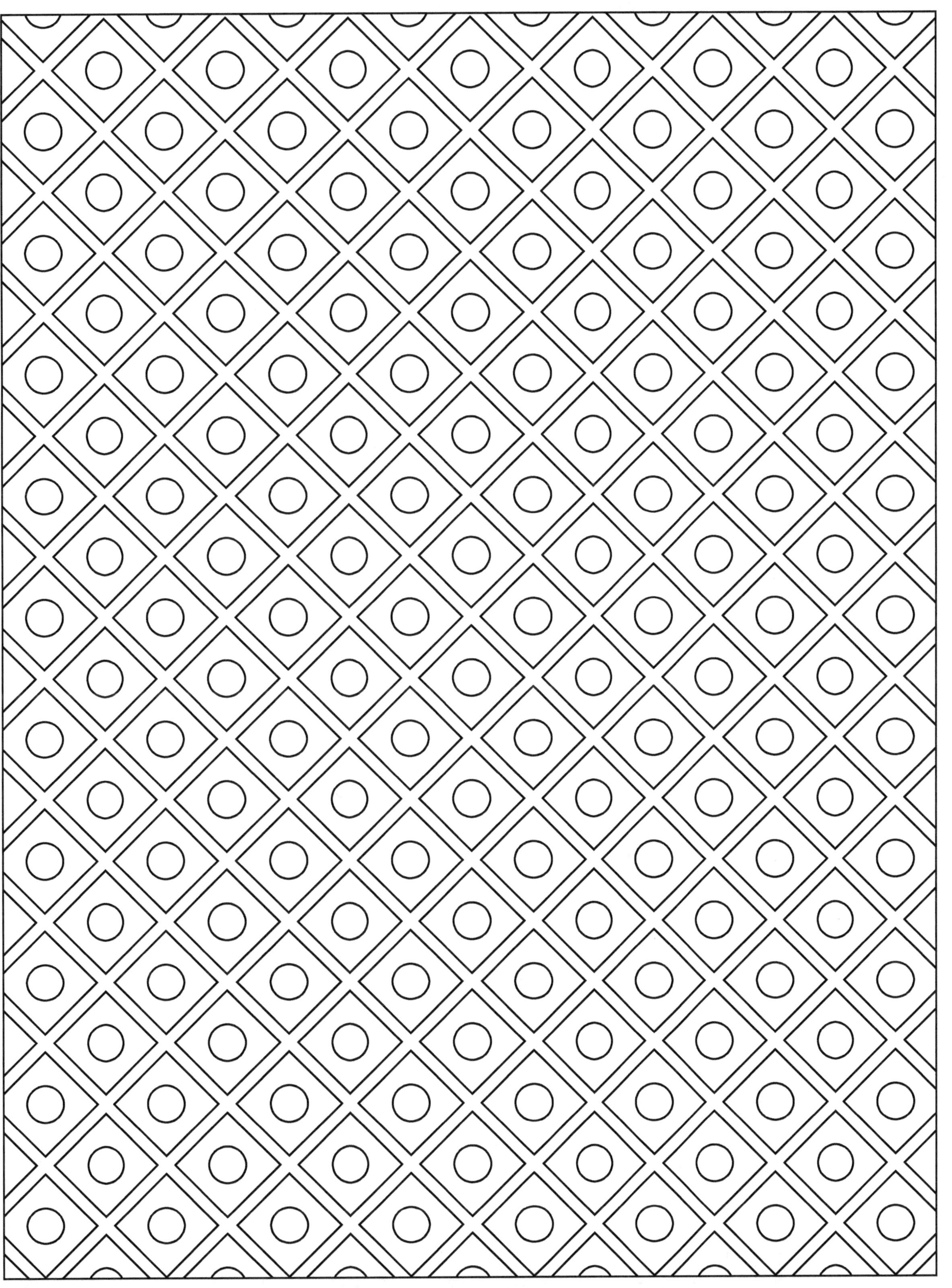

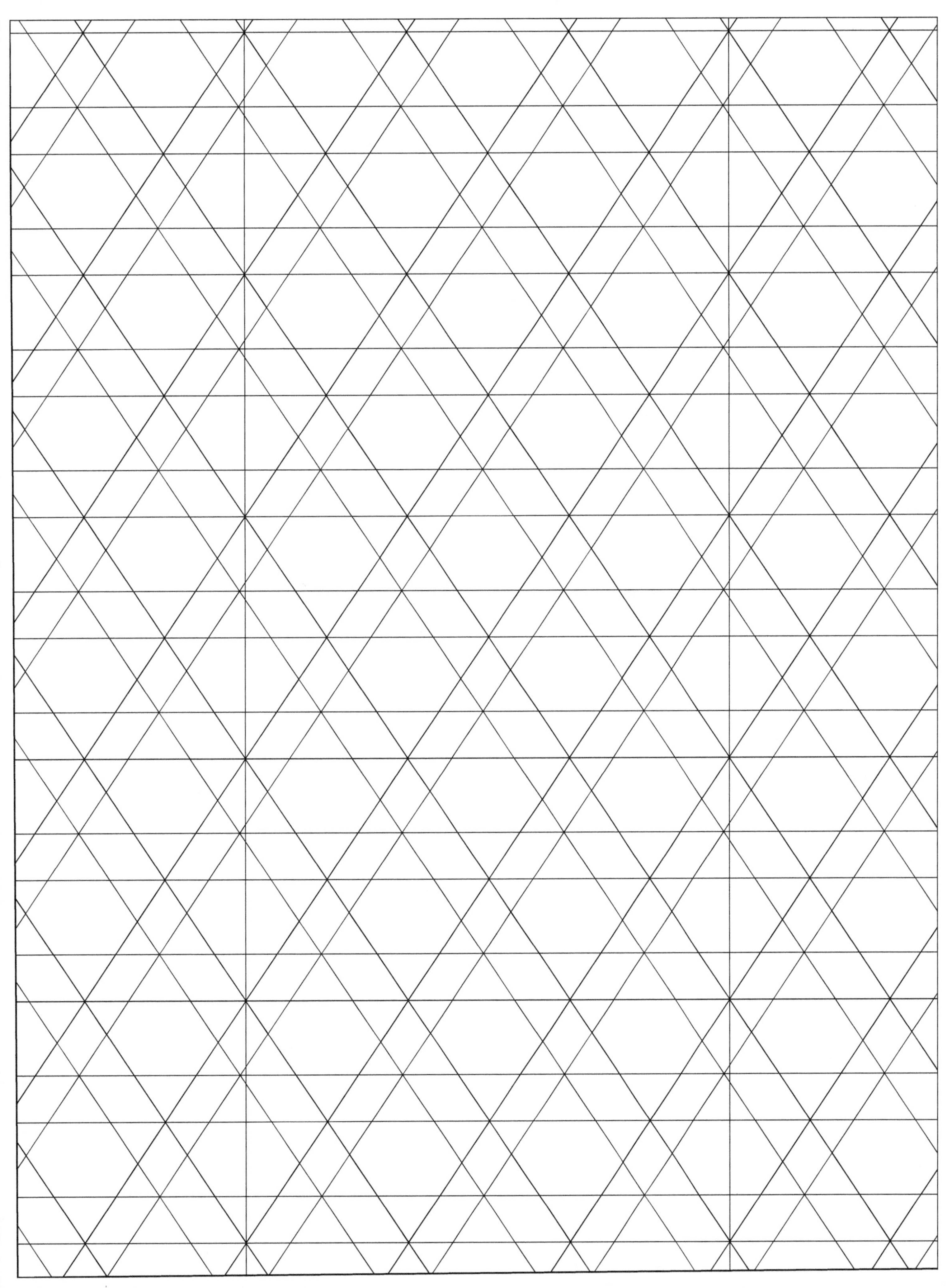

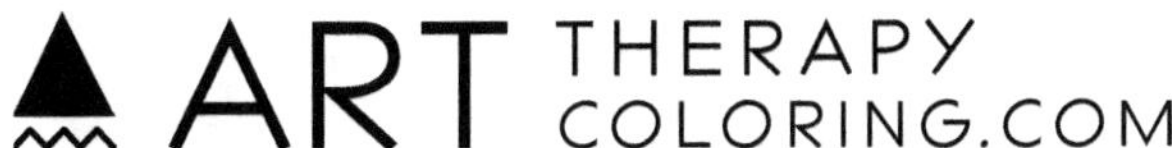

Test Your Colors

Drawings

Drawings

Art Therapy Coloring Books

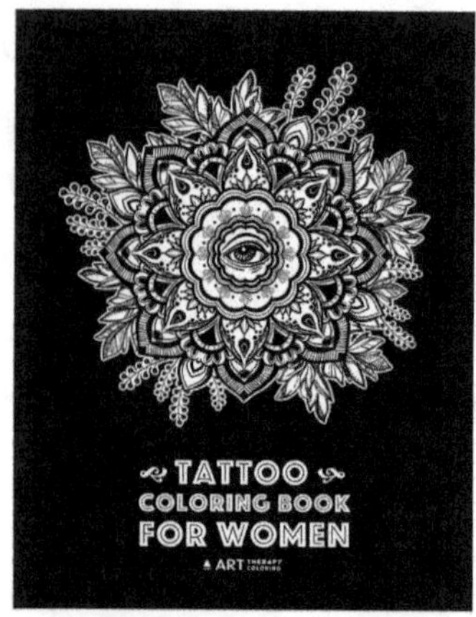
TATTOO
COLORING BOOK
FOR WOMEN

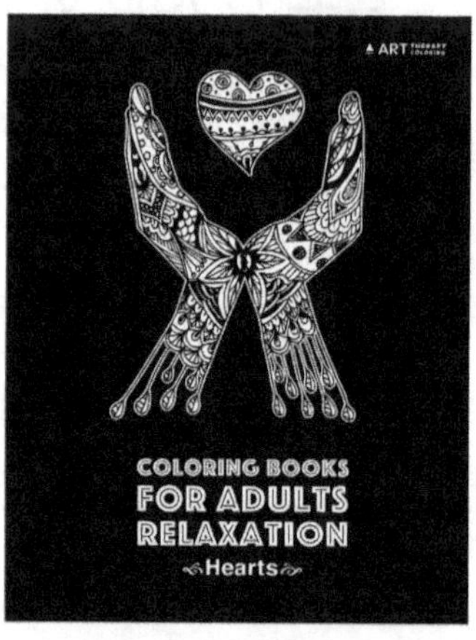
COLORING BOOKS
FOR ADULTS
RELAXATION
Hearts

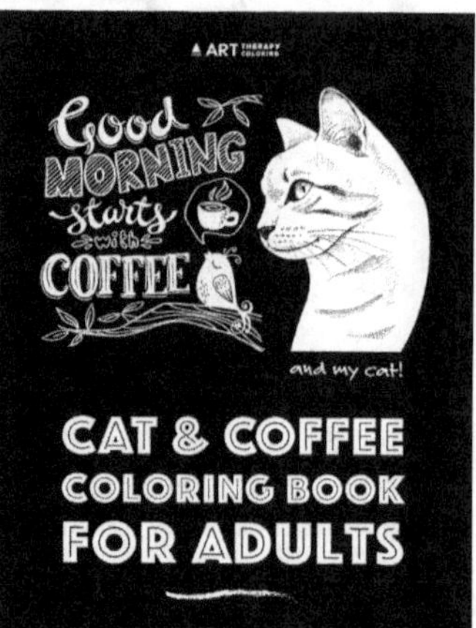
Good
MORNING
starts
with
COFFEE
and my cat!
CAT & COFFEE
COLORING BOOK
FOR ADULTS

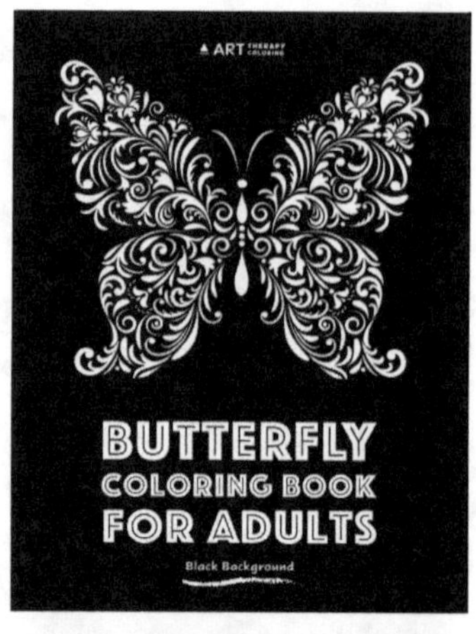
BUTTERFLY
COLORING BOOK
FOR ADULTS
Black Background

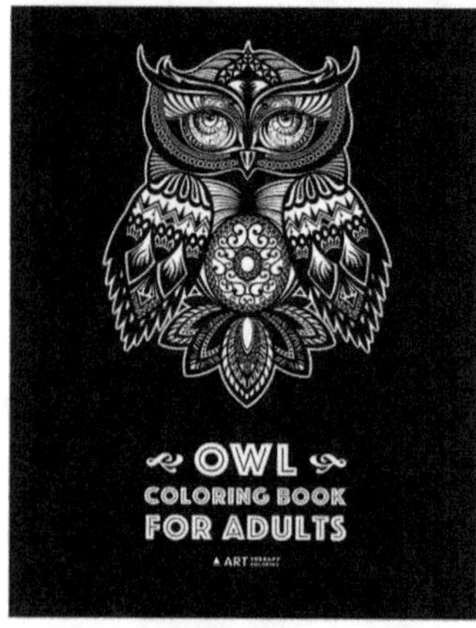
OWL
COLORING BOOK
FOR ADULTS

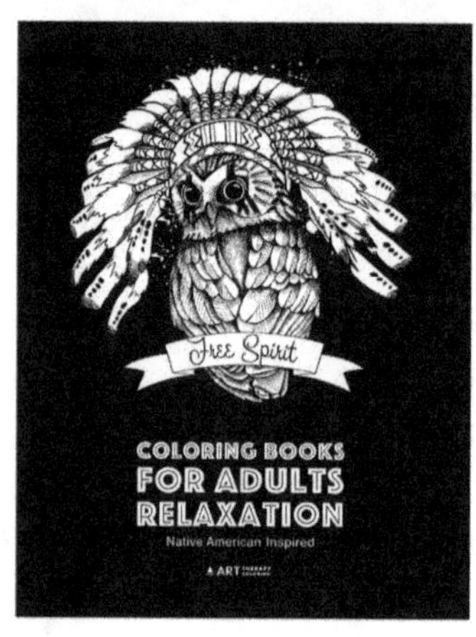
Free Spirit
COLORING BOOKS
FOR ADULTS
RELAXATION
Native American Inspired

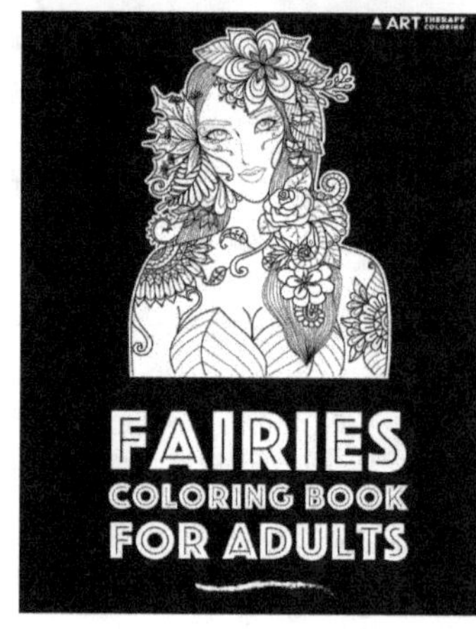
FAIRIES
COLORING BOOK
FOR ADULTS

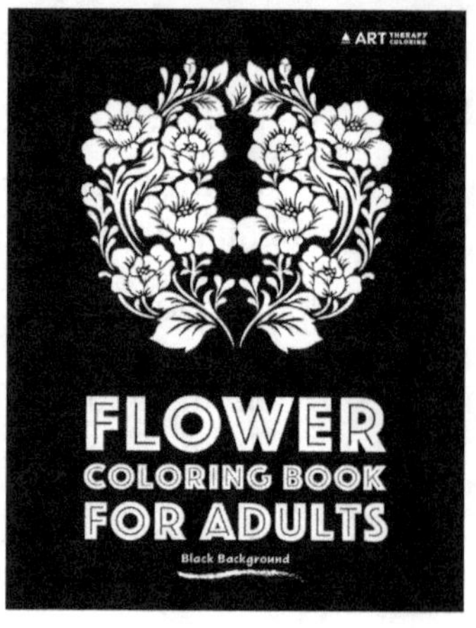
FLOWER
COLORING BOOK
FOR ADULTS
Black Background

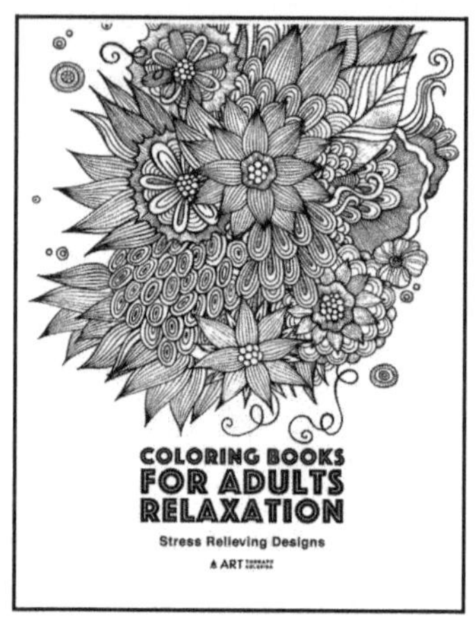
COLORING BOOKS
FOR ADULTS
RELAXATION
Stress Relieving Designs

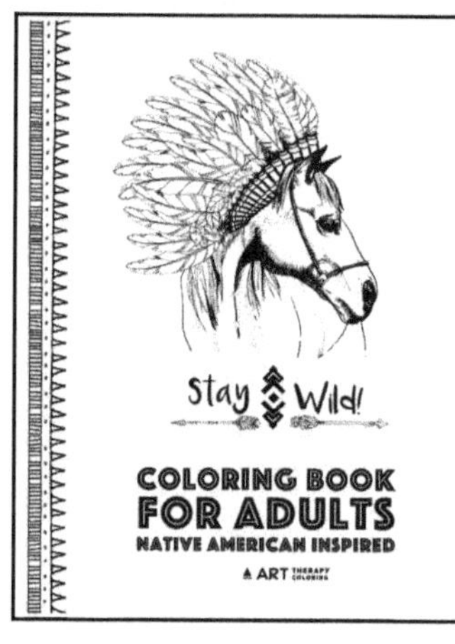
Stay Wild!
COLORING BOOK
FOR ADULTS
NATIVE AMERICAN INSPIRED

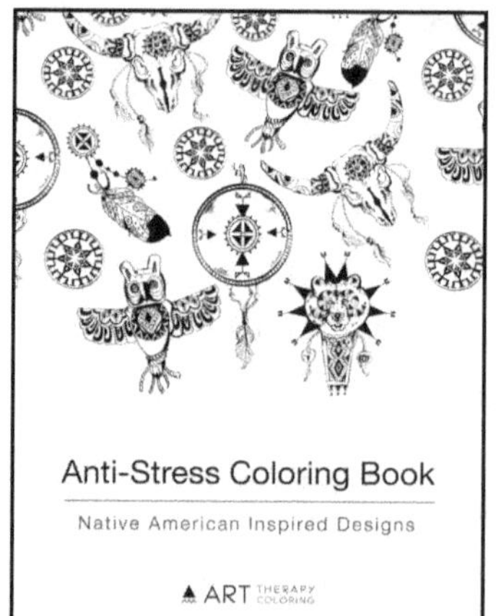
Anti-Stress Coloring Book
Native American Inspired Designs
ART THERAPY COLORING

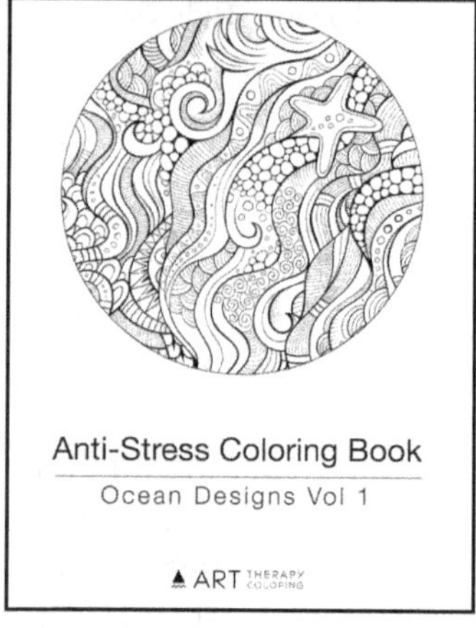
Anti-Stress Coloring Book
Ocean Designs Vol 1
ART THERAPY COLORING

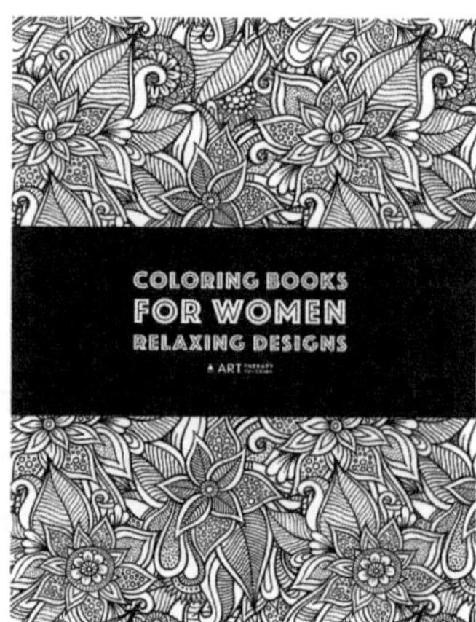
COLORING BOOKS
FOR WOMEN
RELAXING DESIGNS

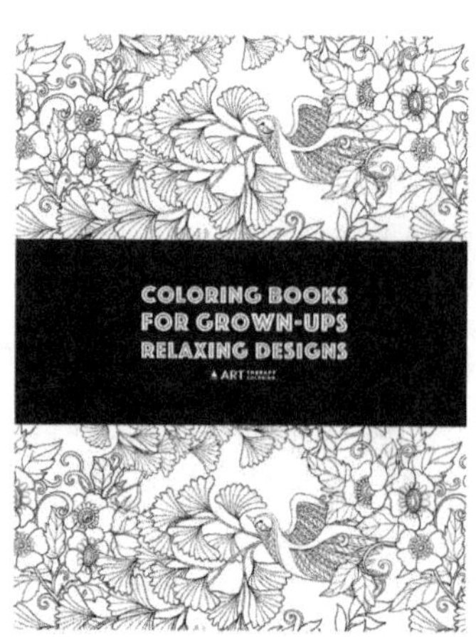
COLORING BOOKS
FOR GROWN-UPS
RELAXING DESIGNS

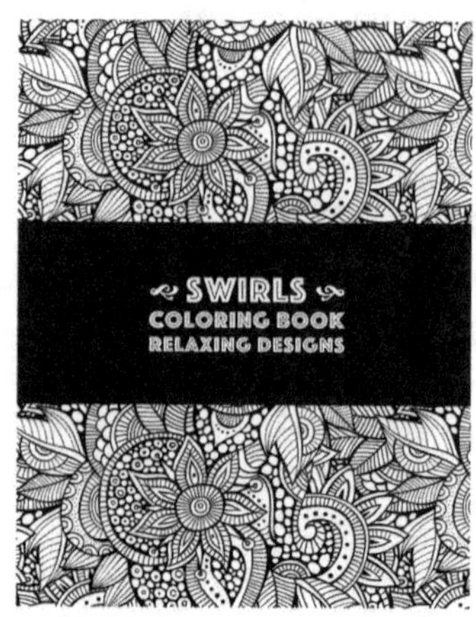
SWIRLS
COLORING BOOK
RELAXING DESIGNS

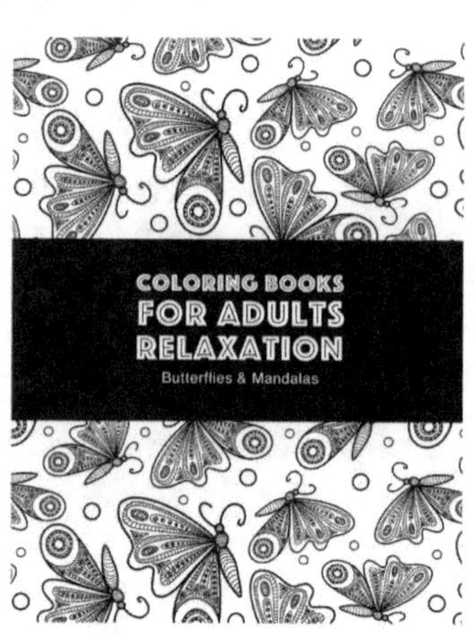
COLORING BOOKS
FOR ADULTS
RELAXATION
Butterflies & Mandalas

Art Therapy Coloring Books

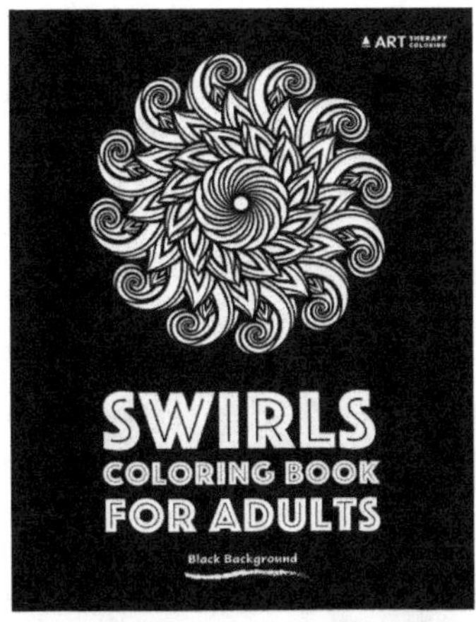

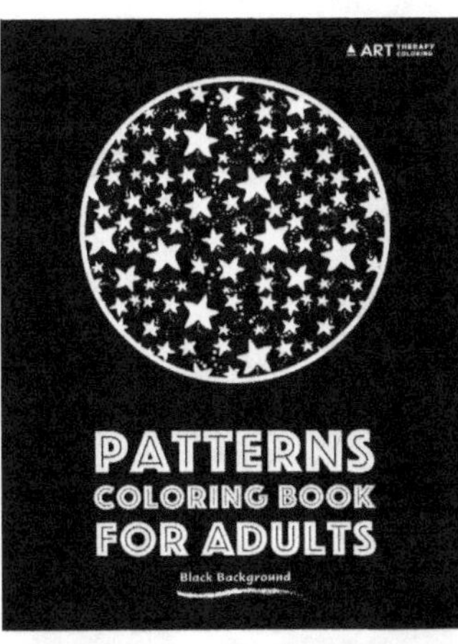

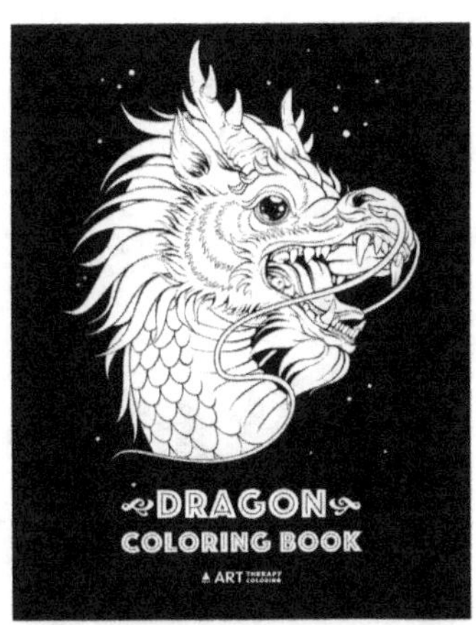

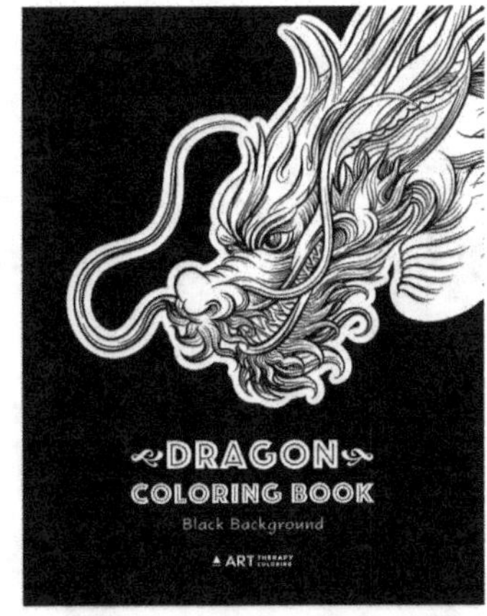

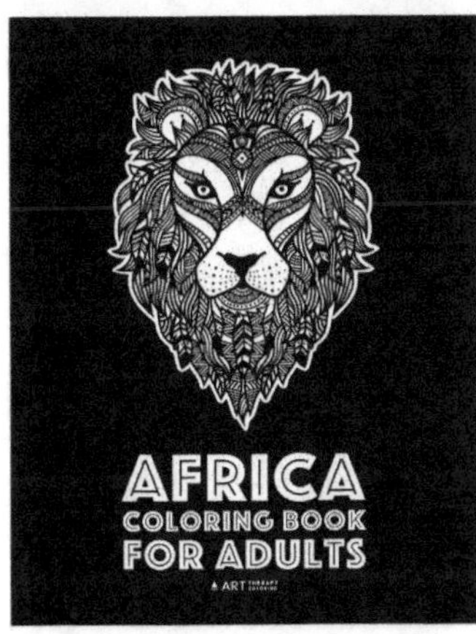

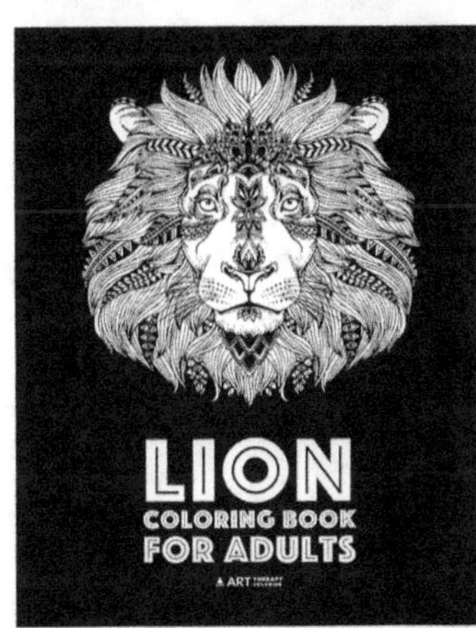

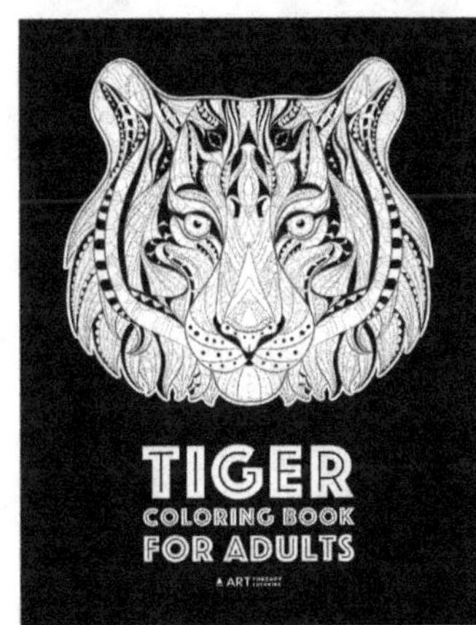

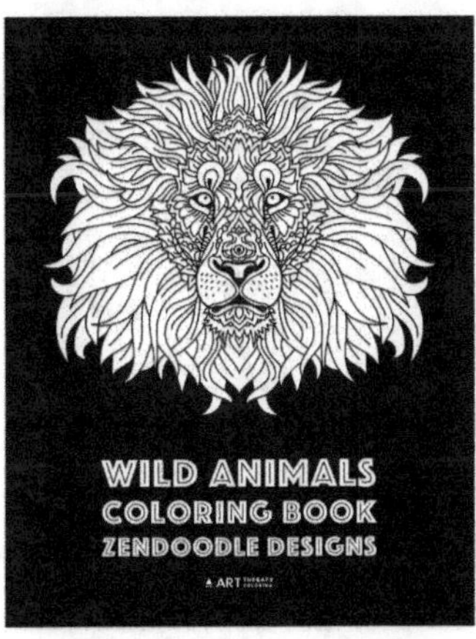

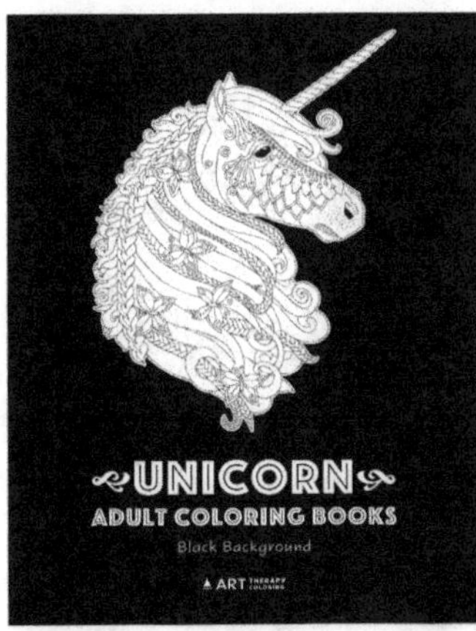

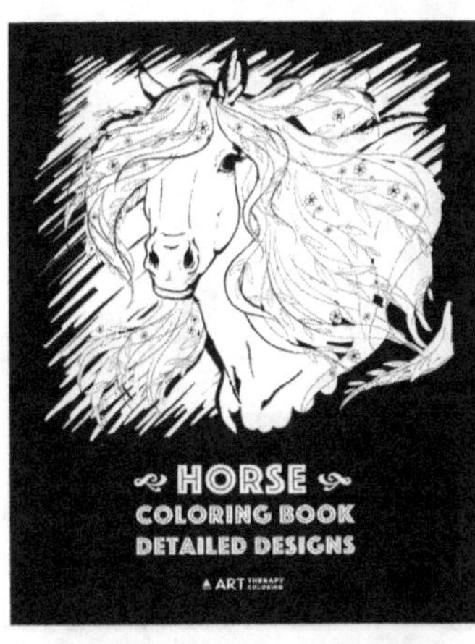

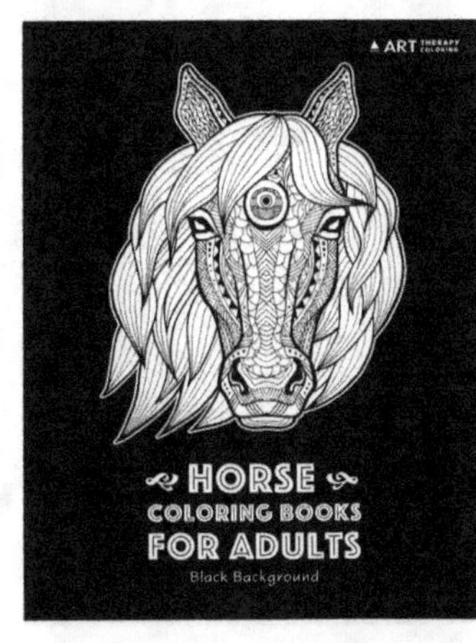

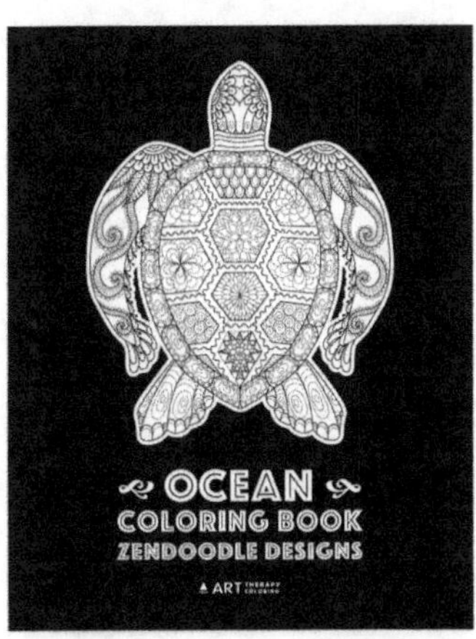

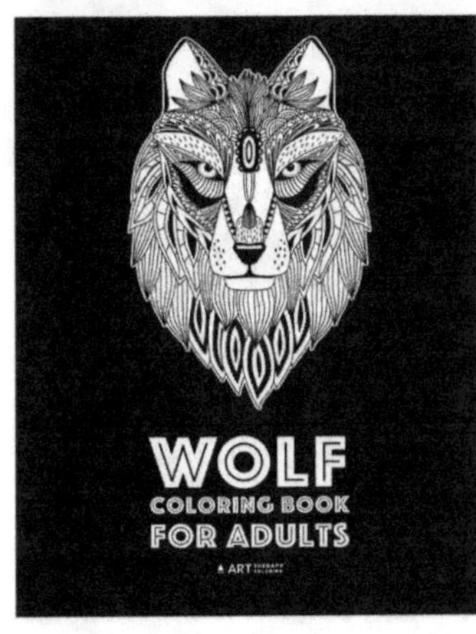

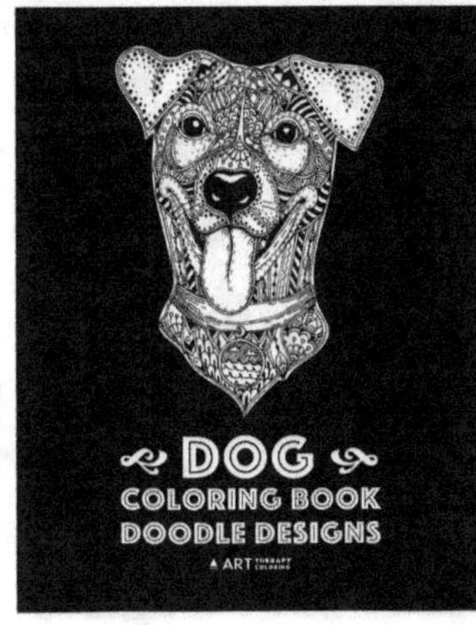

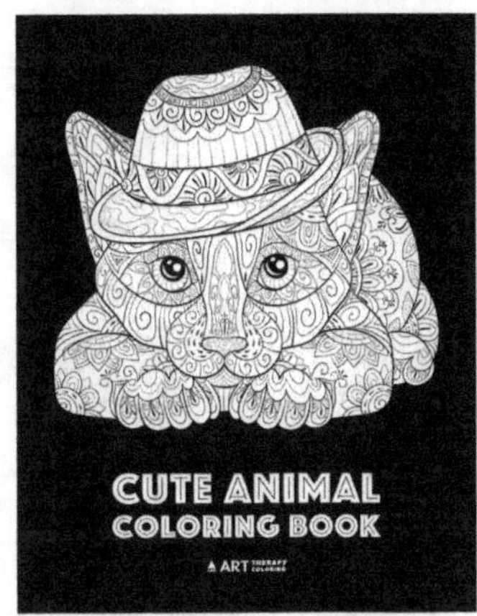

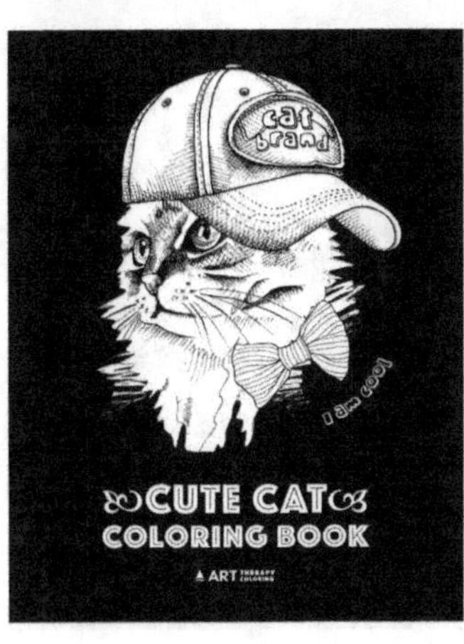

Art Therapy Coloring Books

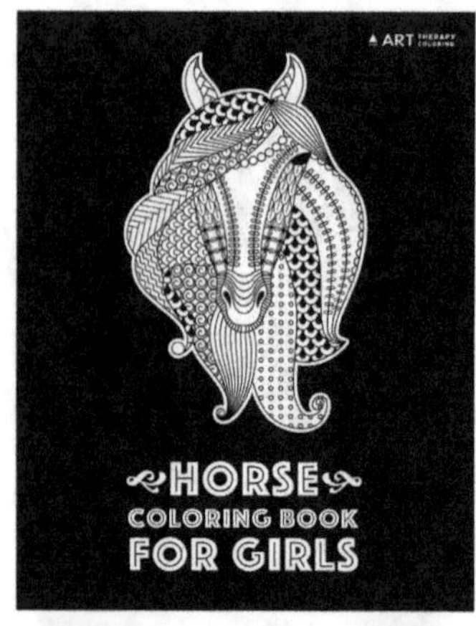
ART THERAPY COLORING
HORSE
COLORING BOOK
FOR GIRLS

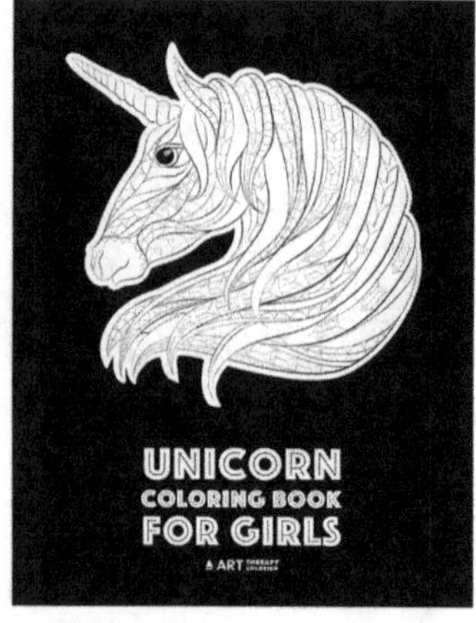
UNICORN
COLORING BOOK
FOR GIRLS

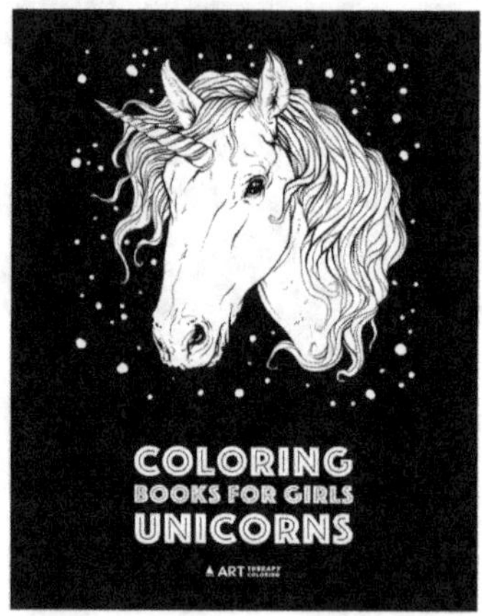
COLORING
BOOKS FOR GIRLS
UNICORNS

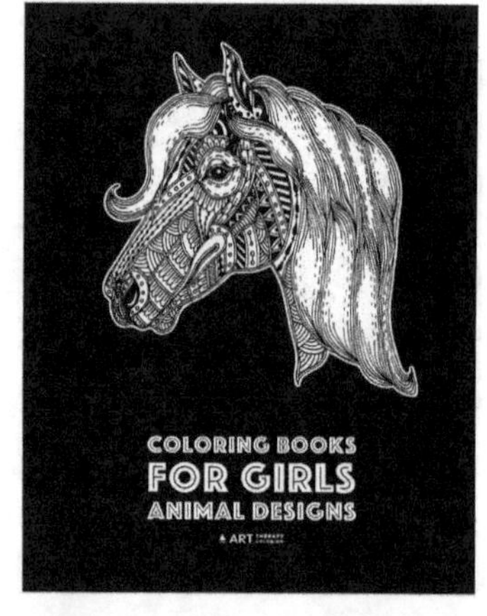
COLORING BOOKS
FOR GIRLS
ANIMAL DESIGNS

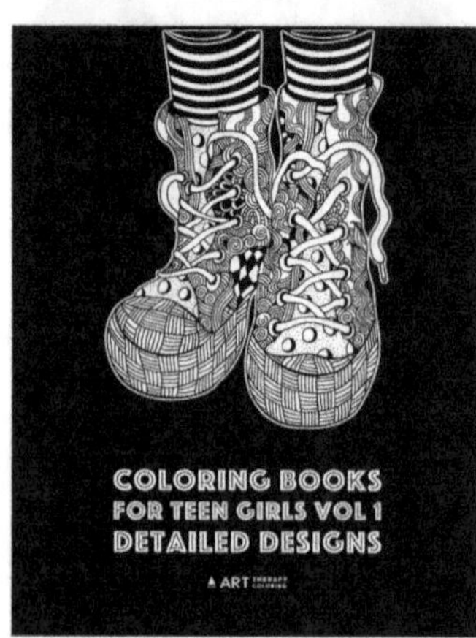
COLORING BOOKS
FOR TEEN GIRLS VOL 1
DETAILED DESIGNS

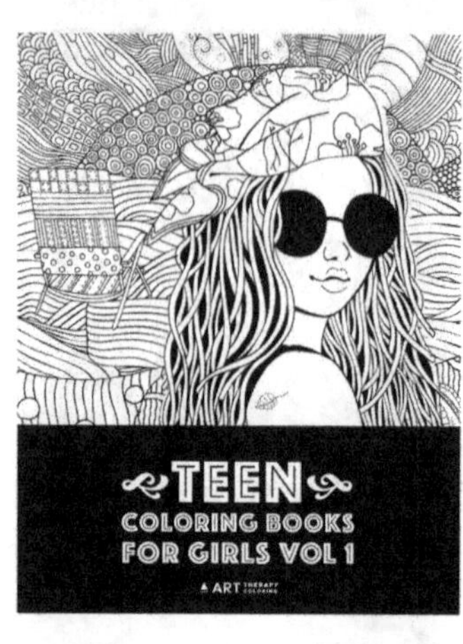
TEEN
COLORING BOOKS
FOR GIRLS VOL 1

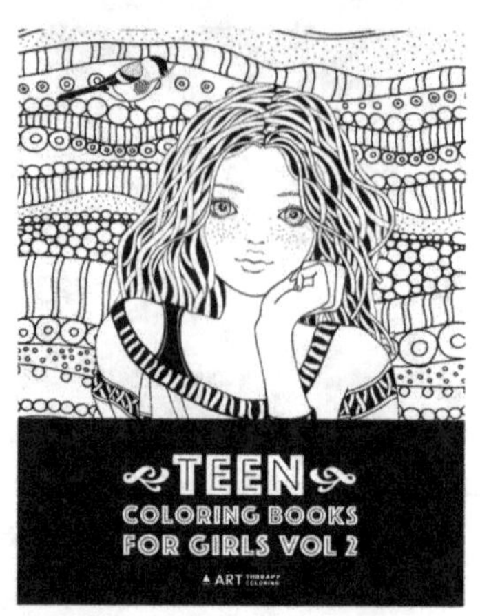
TEEN
COLORING BOOKS
FOR GIRLS VOL 2

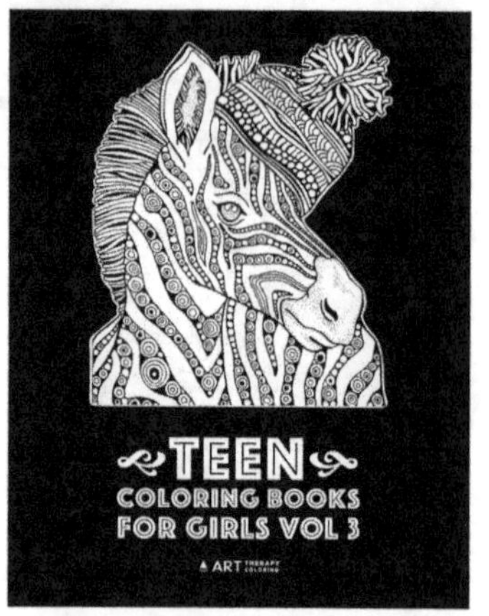
TEEN
COLORING BOOKS
FOR GIRLS VOL 3

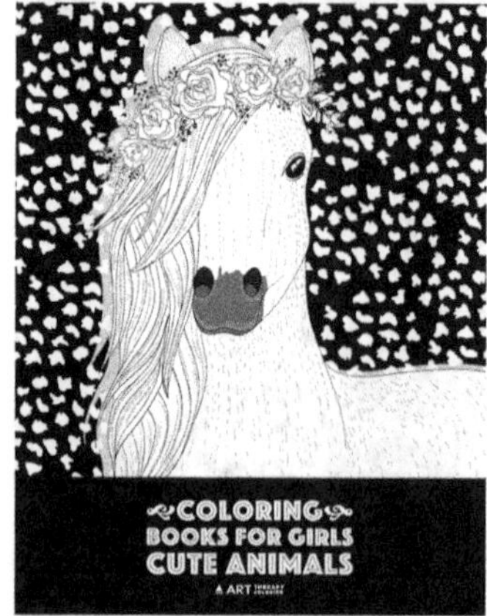
COLORING
BOOKS FOR GIRLS
CUTE ANIMALS

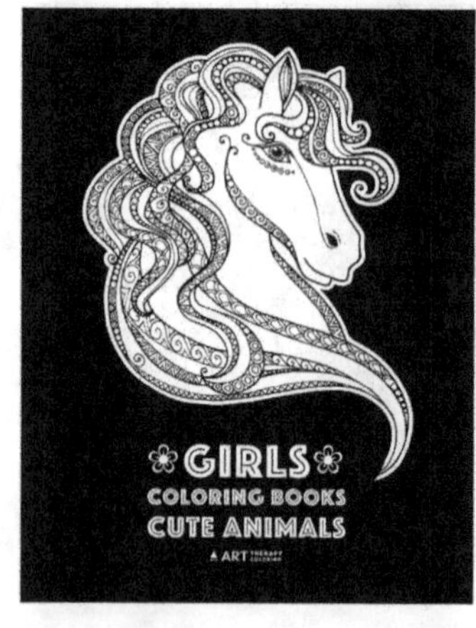
GIRLS
COLORING BOOKS
CUTE ANIMALS

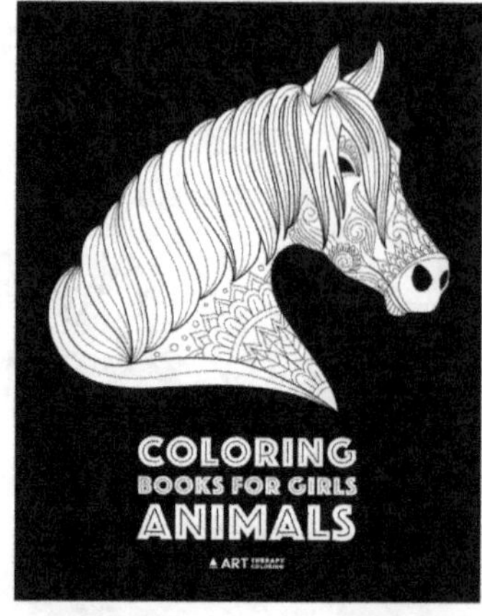
COLORING
BOOKS FOR GIRLS
ANIMALS

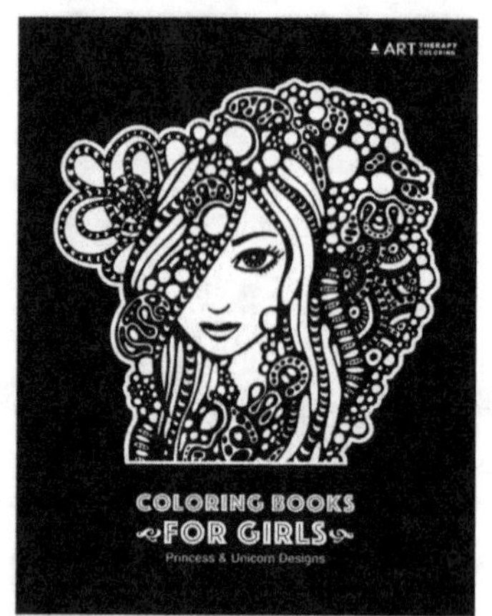
COLORING BOOKS
FOR GIRLS
Princess & Unicorn Designs

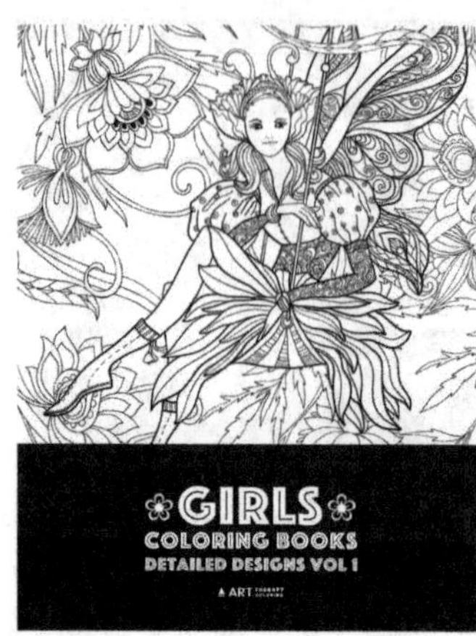
GIRLS
COLORING BOOKS
DETAILED DESIGNS VOL 1

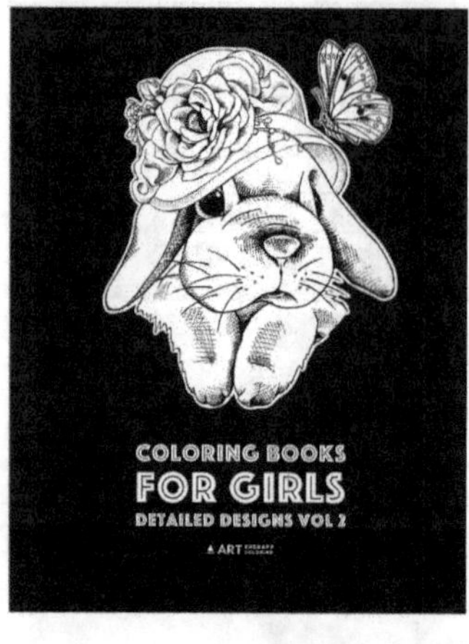
COLORING BOOKS
FOR GIRLS
DETAILED DESIGNS VOL 2

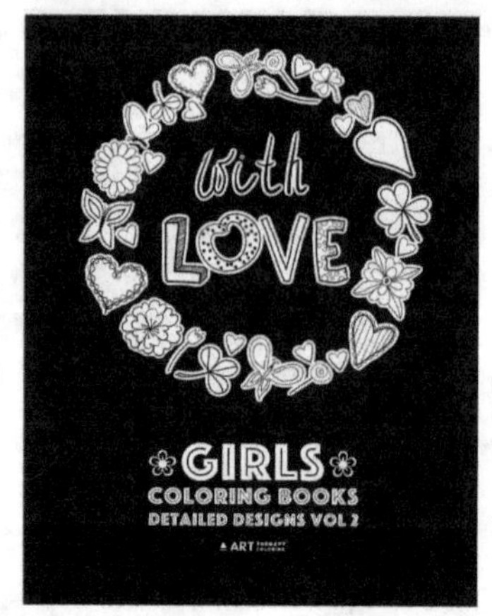
With
LOVE
GIRLS
COLORING BOOKS
DETAILED DESIGNS VOL 2

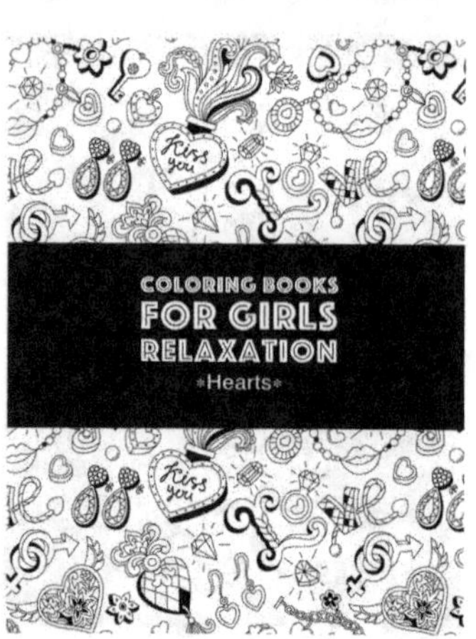
COLORING BOOKS
FOR GIRLS
RELAXATION
Hearts

Art Therapy Coloring Books

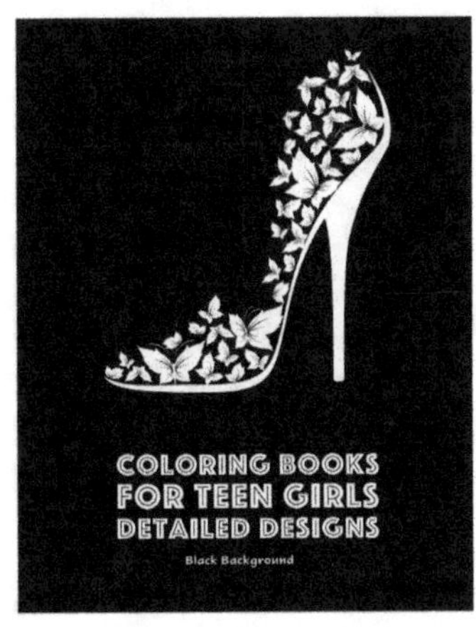

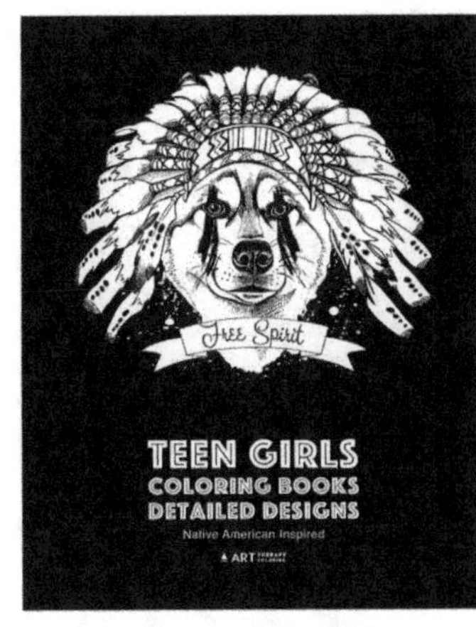

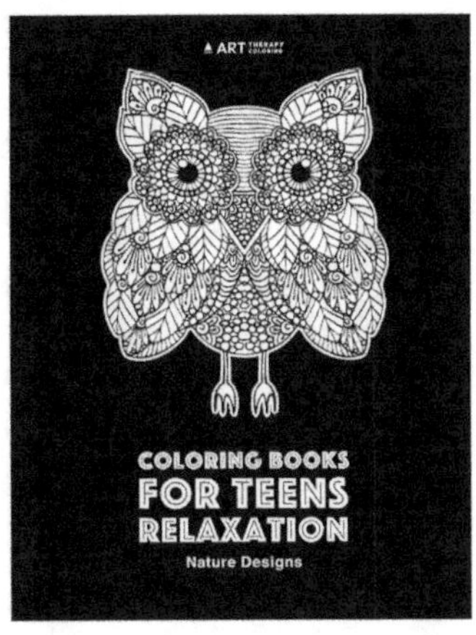

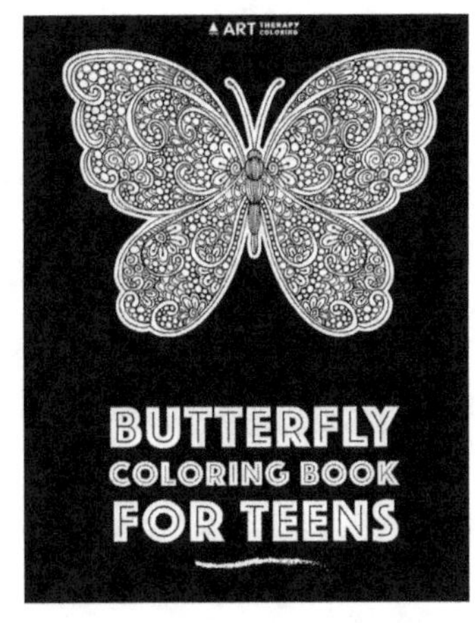

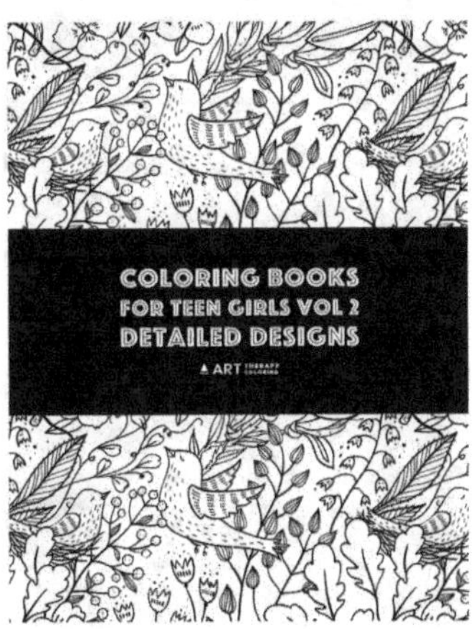

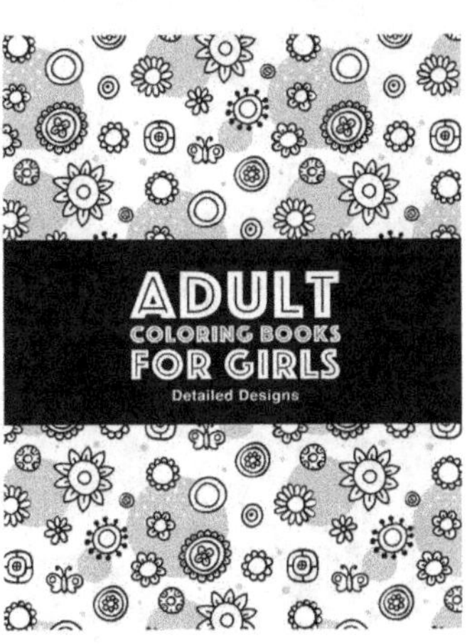

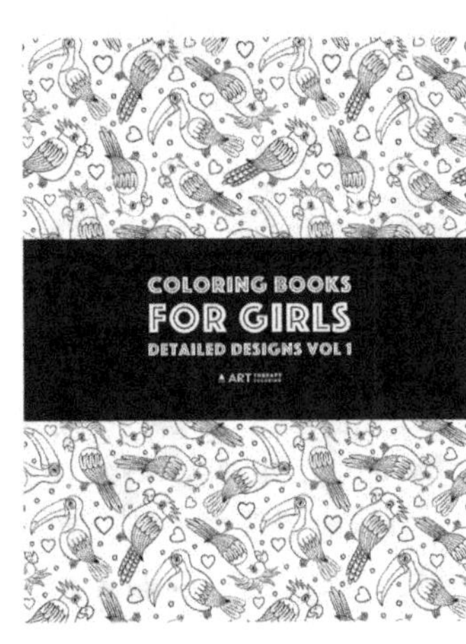

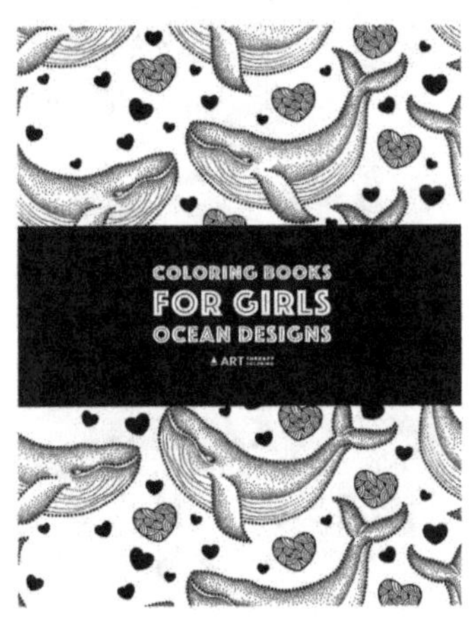

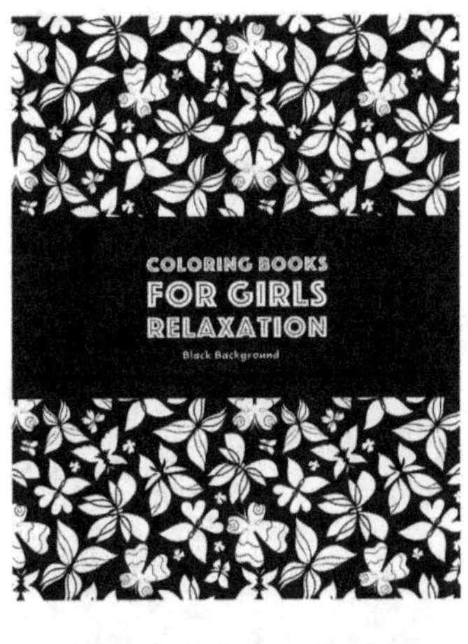

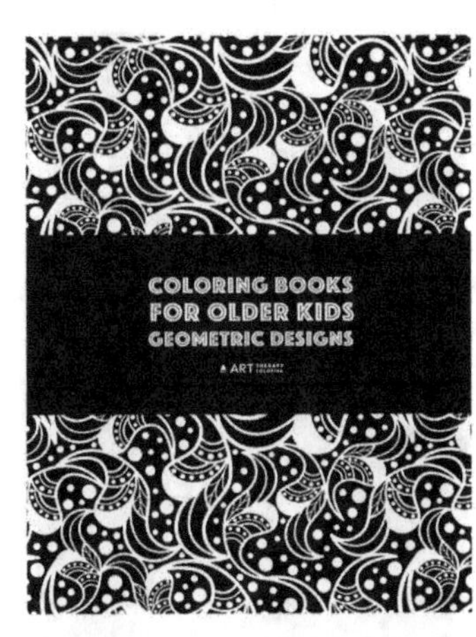

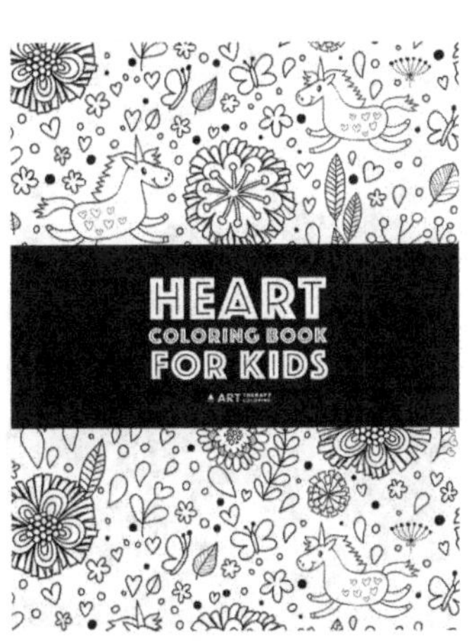

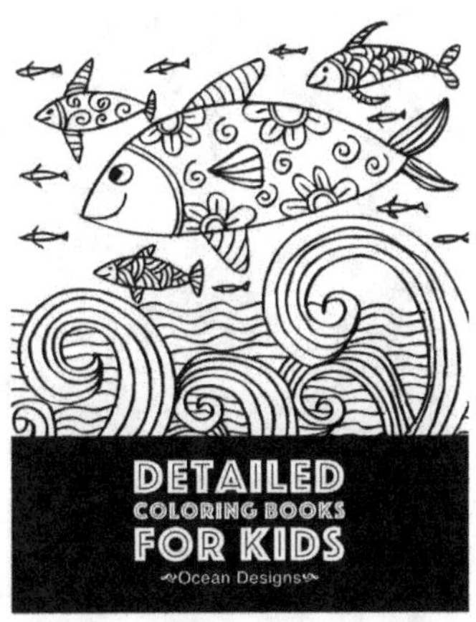

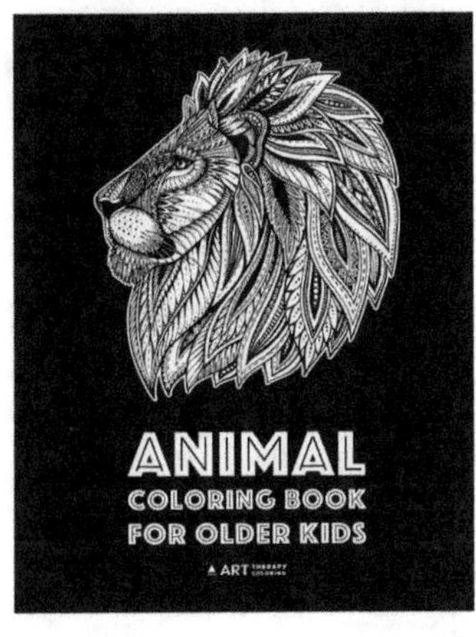

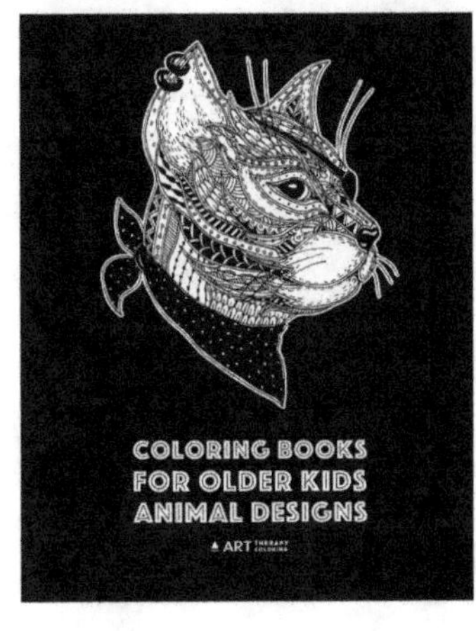

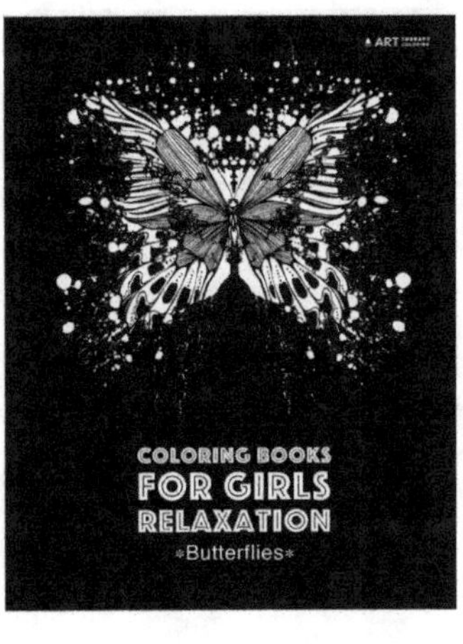

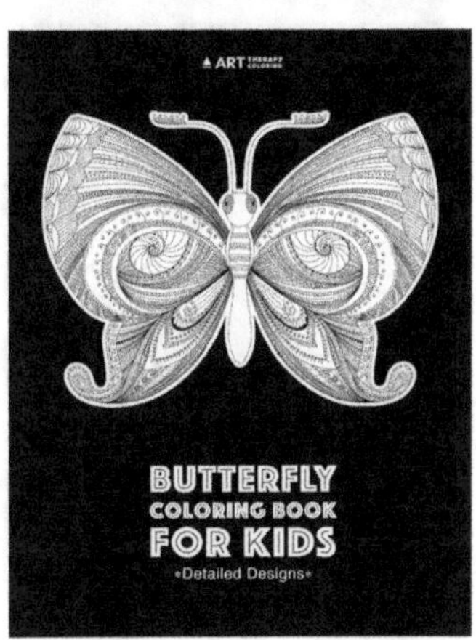

Art Therapy Coloring Books

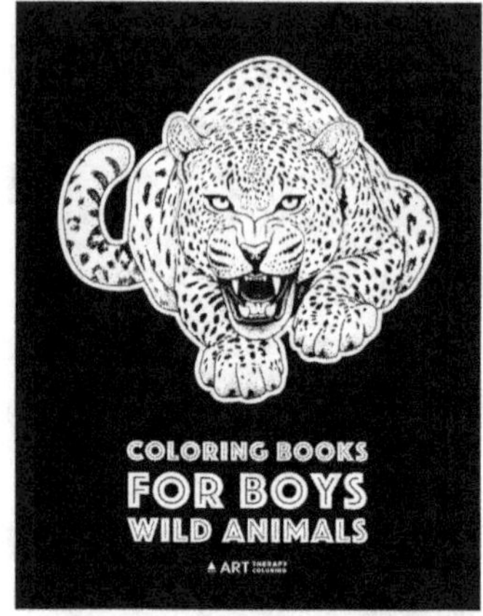
COLORING BOOKS
FOR BOYS
WILD ANIMALS
ART

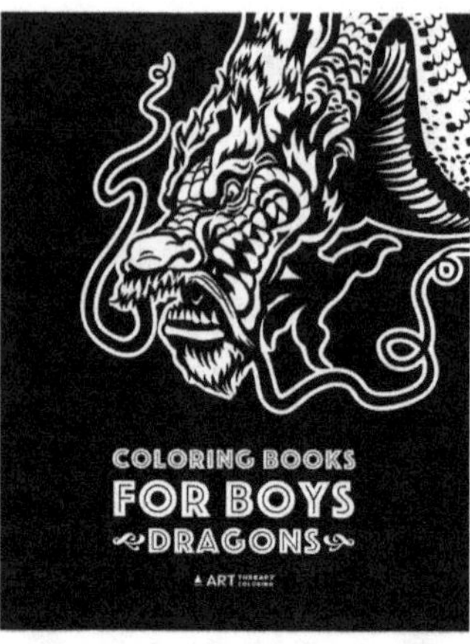
COLORING BOOKS
FOR BOYS
DRAGONS
ART

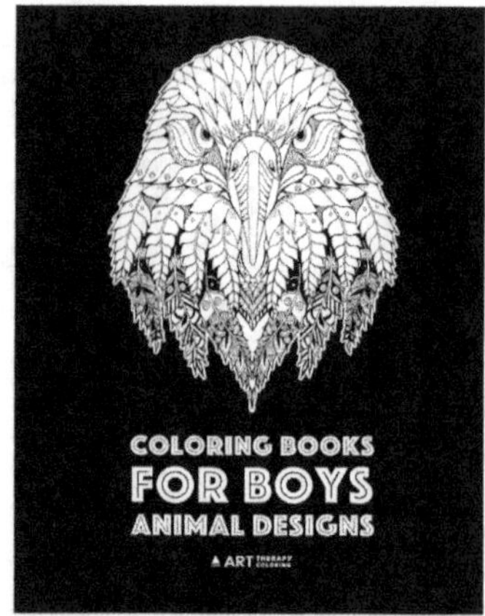
COLORING BOOKS
FOR BOYS
ANIMAL DESIGNS
ART

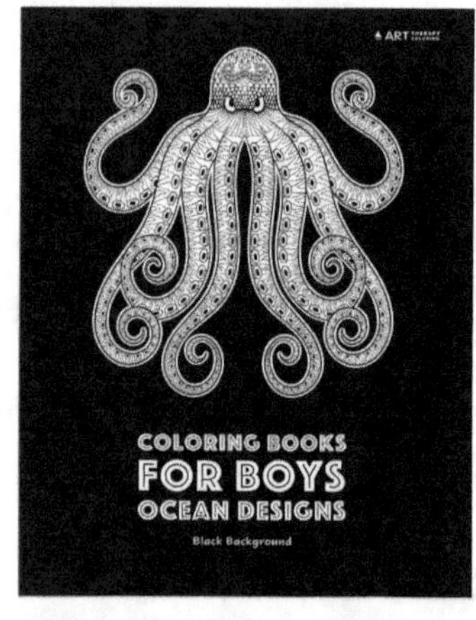
ART
COLORING BOOKS
FOR BOYS
OCEAN DESIGNS
Black Background

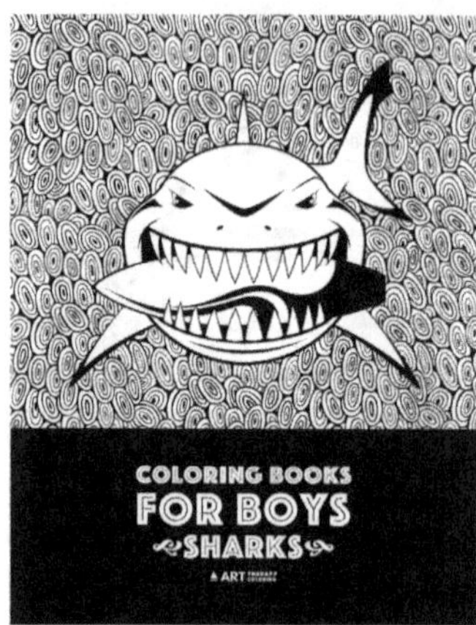
COLORING BOOKS
FOR BOYS
SHARKS
ART

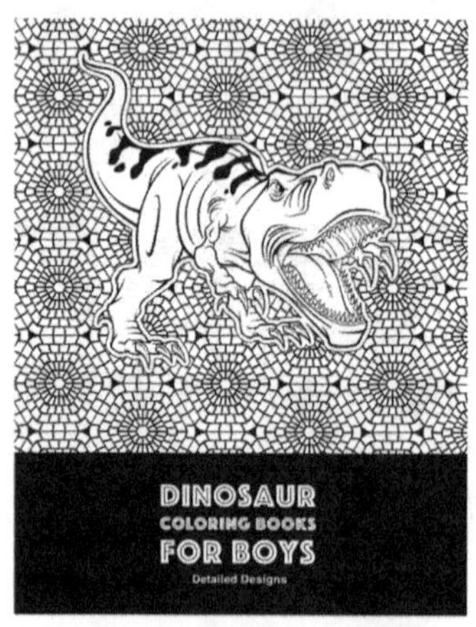
DINOSAUR
COLORING BOOKS
FOR BOYS
Detailed Designs

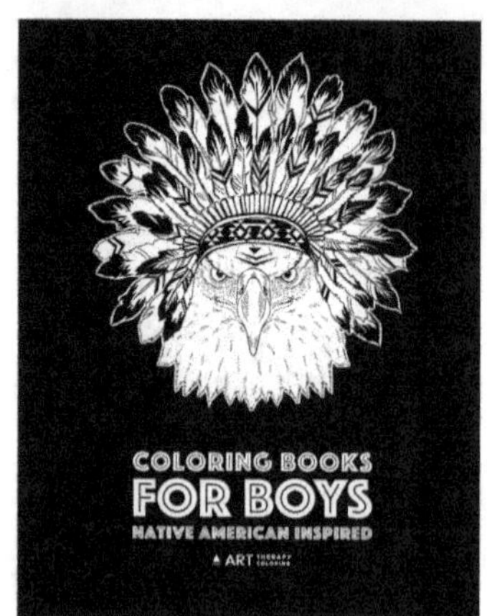
COLORING BOOKS
FOR BOYS
NATIVE AMERICAN INSPIRED
ART

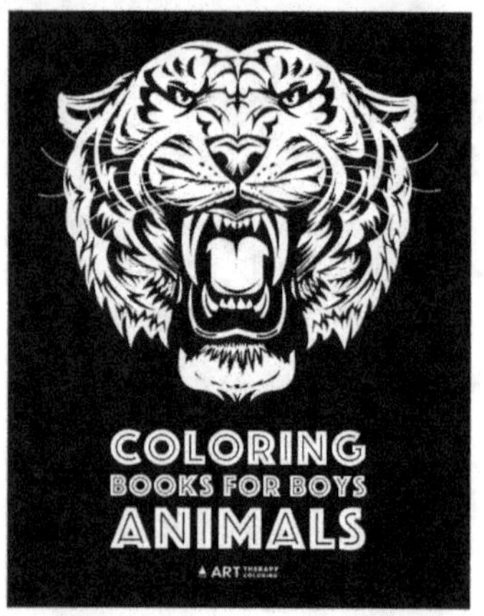
COLORING
BOOKS FOR BOYS
ANIMALS
ART

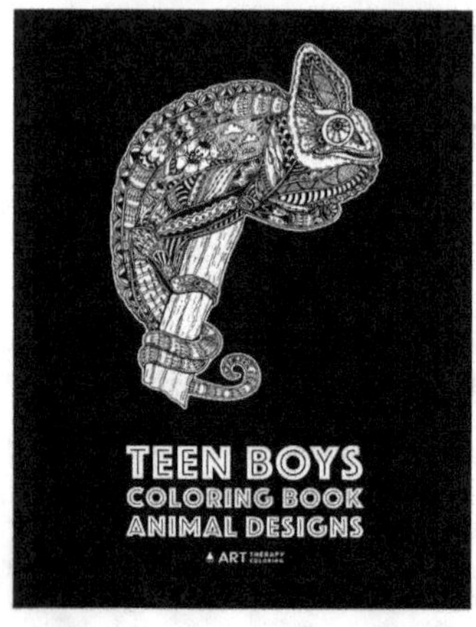
TEEN BOYS
COLORING BOOK
ANIMAL DESIGNS
ART

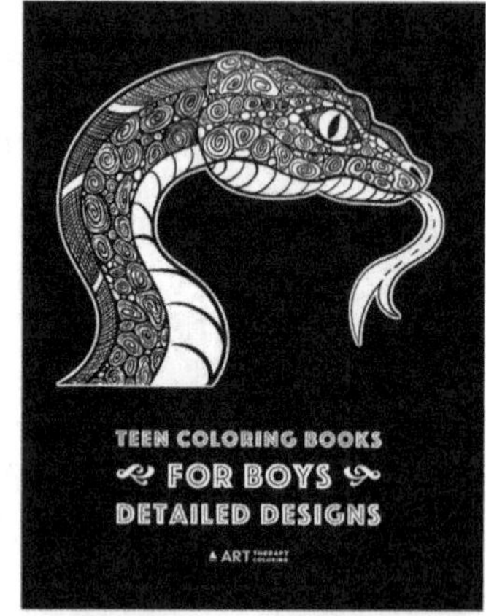
TEEN COLORING BOOKS
FOR BOYS
DETAILED DESIGNS
ART

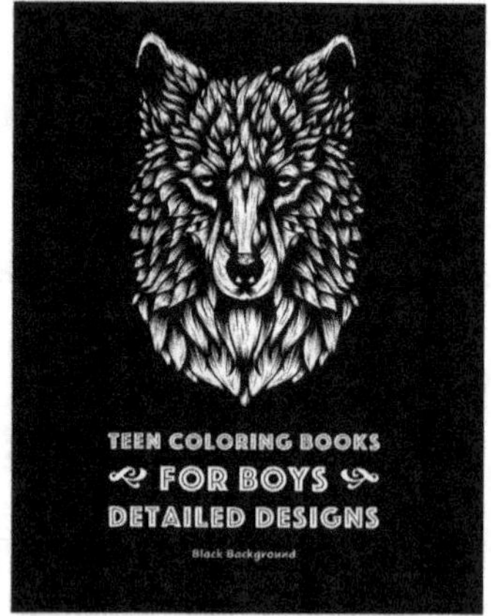
TEEN COLORING BOOKS
FOR BOYS
DETAILED DESIGNS
Black Background

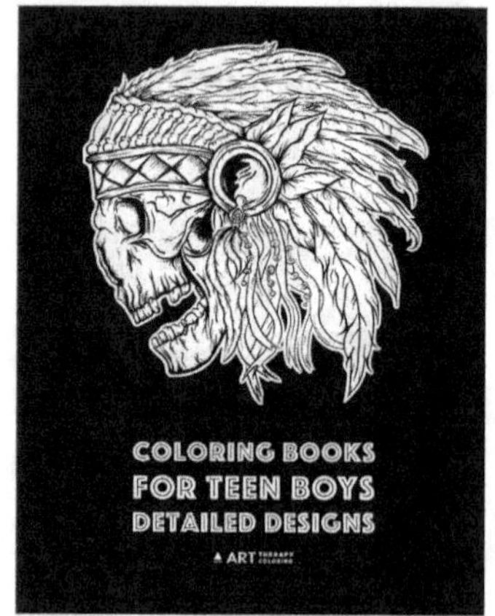
COLORING BOOKS
FOR TEEN BOYS
DETAILED DESIGNS
ART

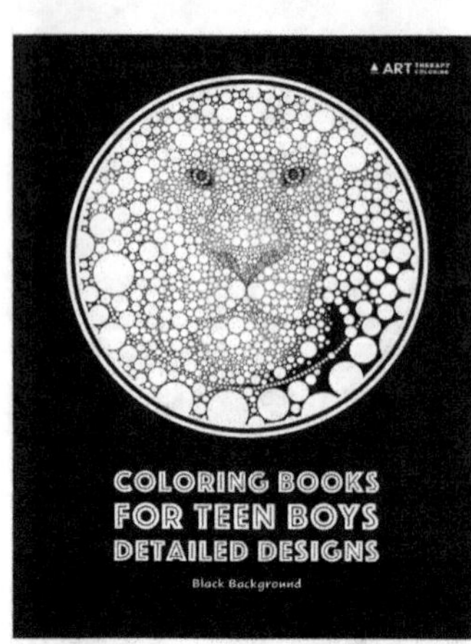
ART
COLORING BOOKS
FOR TEEN BOYS
DETAILED DESIGNS
Black Background

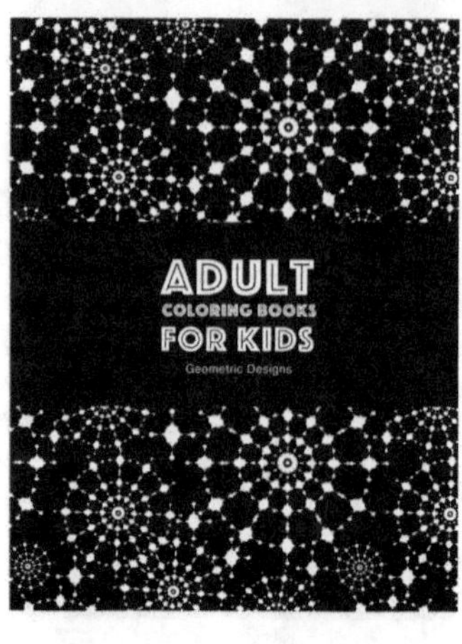
ADULT
COLORING BOOKS
FOR KIDS
Geometric Designs

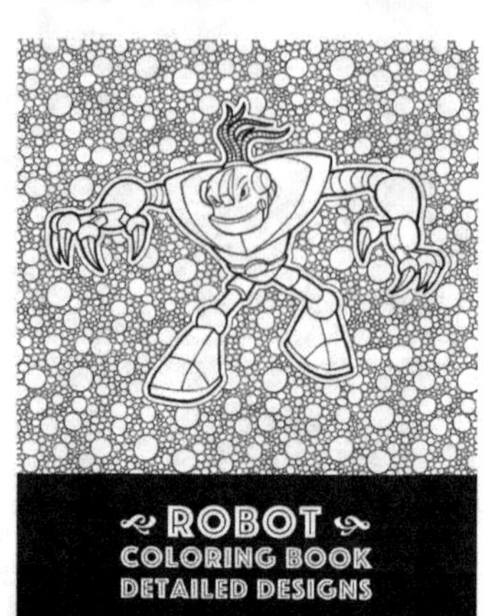
ROBOT
COLORING BOOK
DETAILED DESIGNS

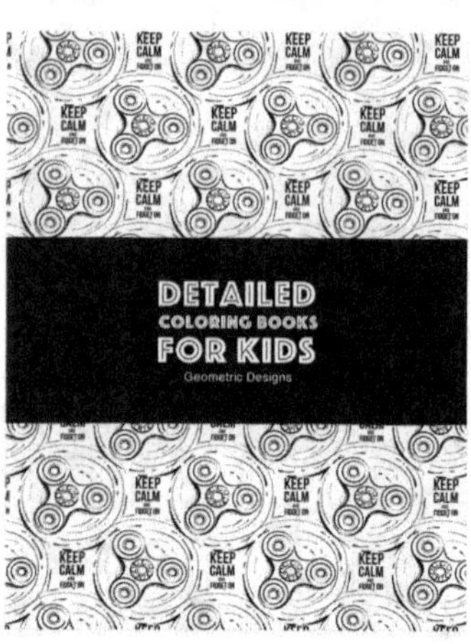
DETAILED
COLORING BOOKS
FOR KIDS
Geometric Designs

Art Therapy Coloring Books

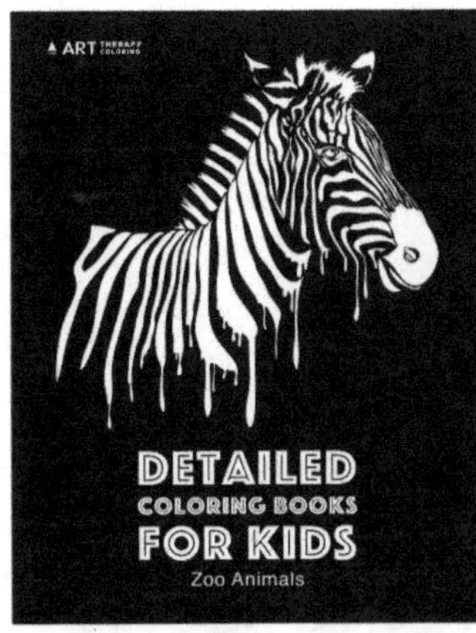

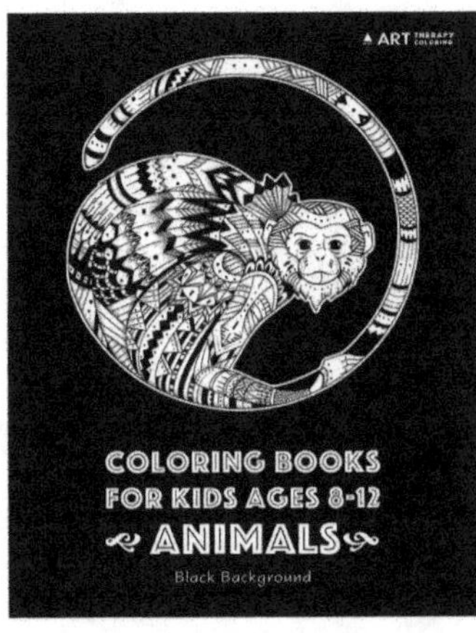

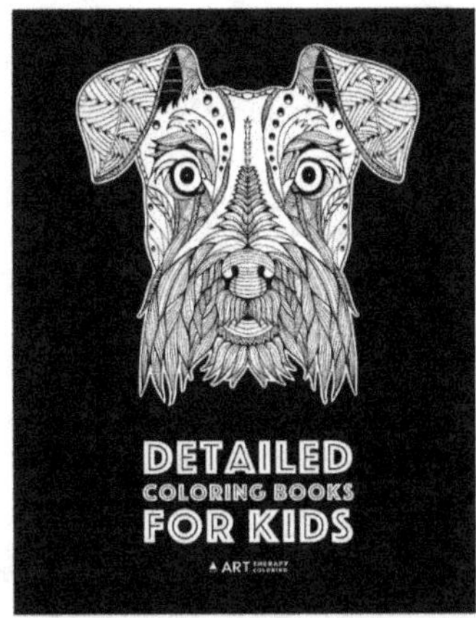

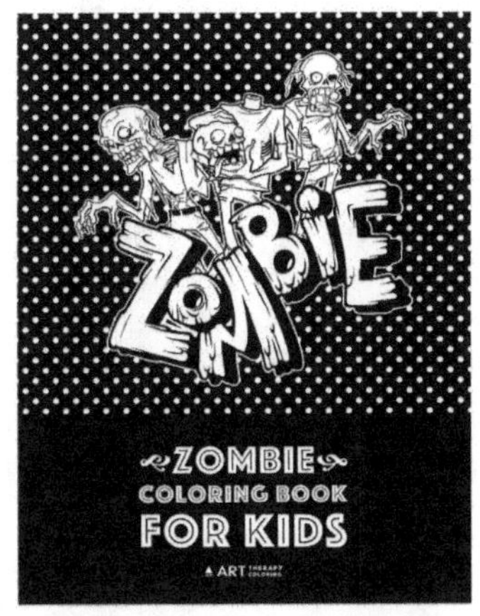

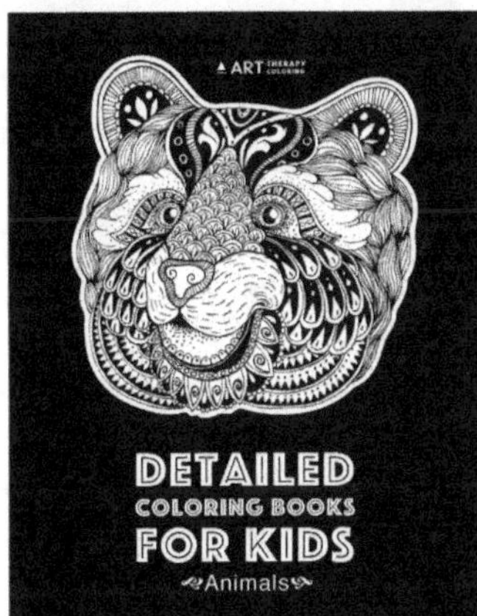

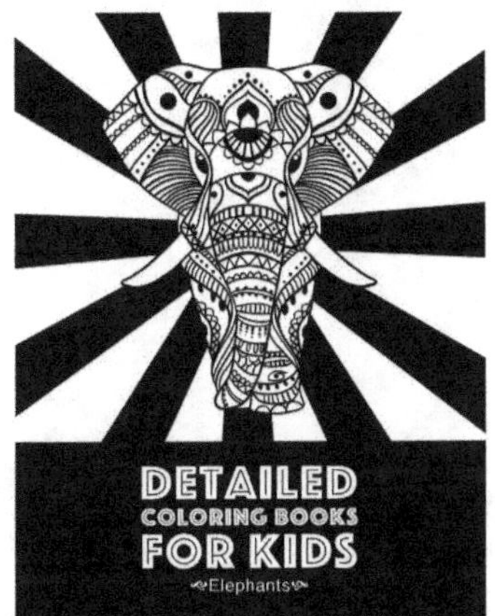

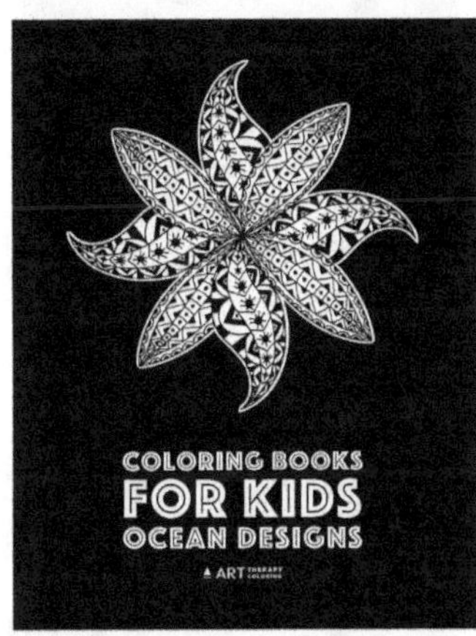

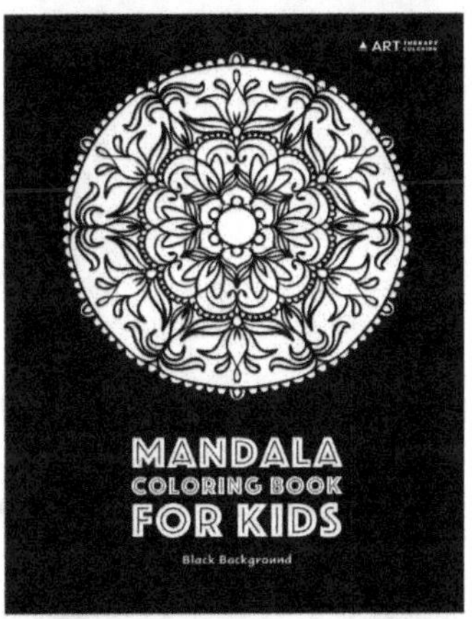

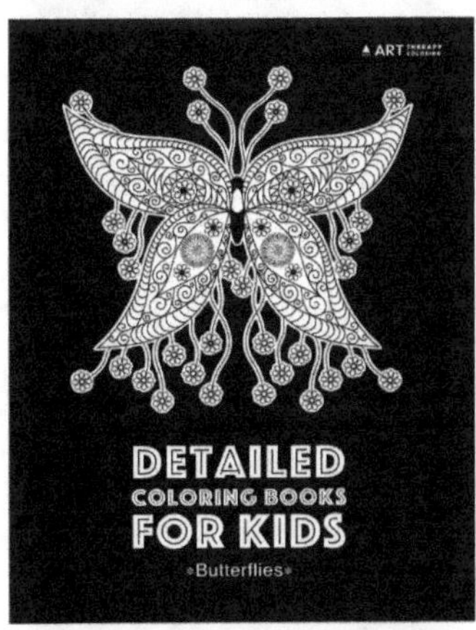

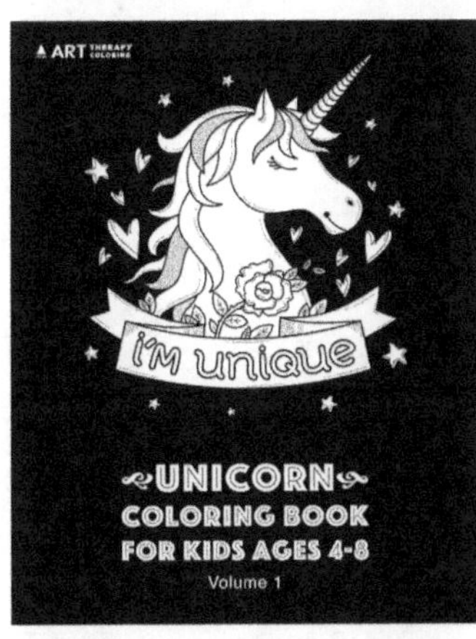

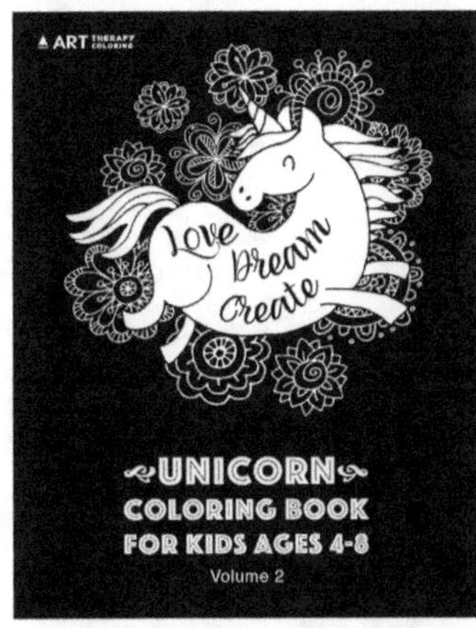

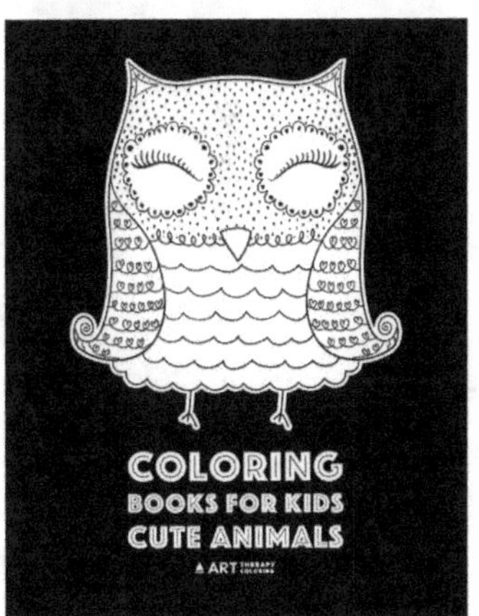

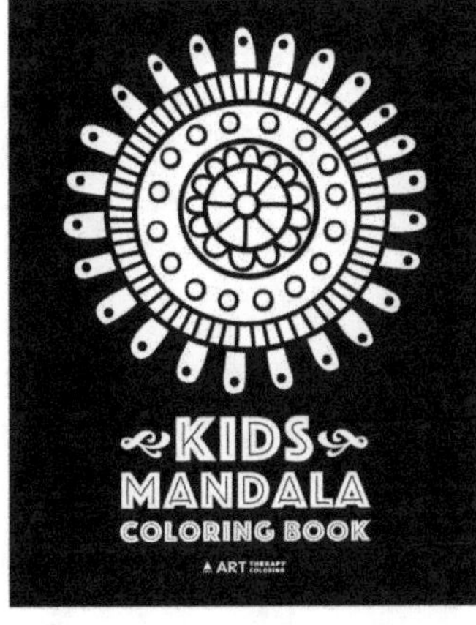

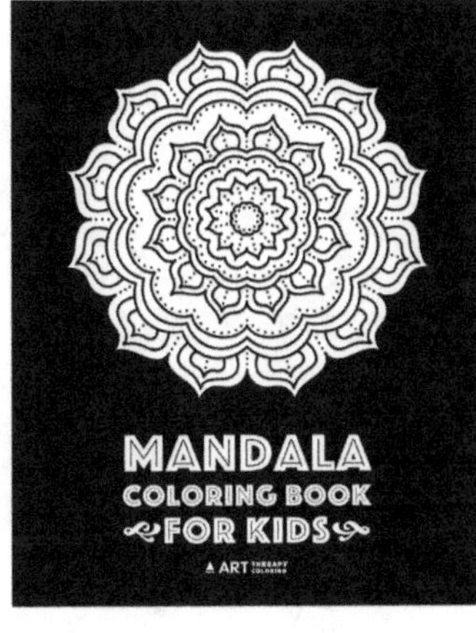

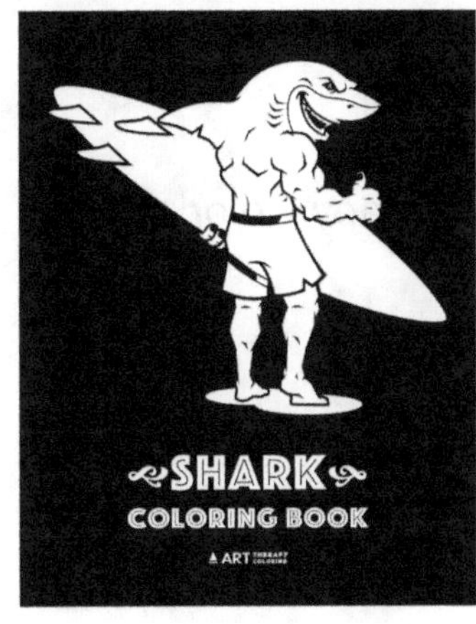

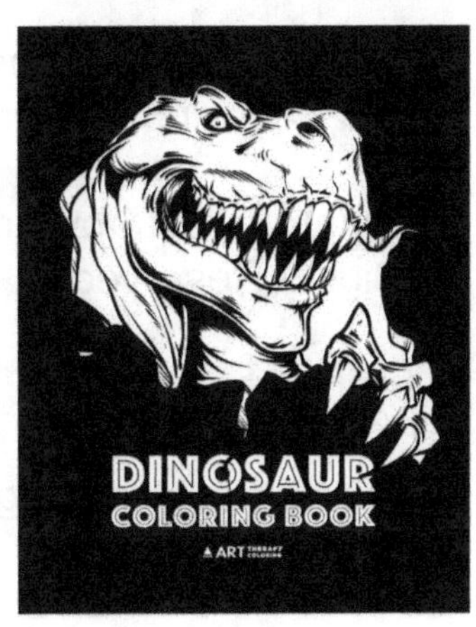

Geometric Coloring Book
Stress Relieving Designs Vol 1

Published by:
Art Therapy Coloring
www.arttherapycoloring.com

ISBN: 978-1-944427-26-9

www.ingramcontent.com/pod-product-compliance
Lightning Source LLC
LaVergne TN
LVHW080336110826
845155LV00027B/251
* 9 7 8 1 9 4 4 4 2 7 2 6 9 *